TEACHING

WITH

BRAVERY

Meditation and Heart Advice for Teachers

NOEL MCLELLAN

ARCHWAY
PUBLISHING

Archway Publishing books may be ordered through booksellers or by contacting:

Archway Publishing
1663 Liberty Drive
Bloomington, IN 47403
www.archwaypublishing.com
1 (888) 242-5904

ISBN: 978-1-4808-7229-5 (sc)
ISBN: 978-1-4808-7230-1 (e)

Print information available on the last page.

Archway Publishing rev. date: 12/06/2018

Contents

Part IV: Teaching Like the Sun

Part V: Touching the Earth

Homage to Manjushri, Youthful Glory of Learning

Introduction

One afternoon when I was in sixth grade, as I was leaving school for the day the principal stopped me at the door, took my hand, and with a gentle and direct look said, "Every day I see you becoming more of a young prince, a gentleman, and a warrior." I didn't really think much about it at the time. I replied with an eloquent, "Uh, okay," and went on my way. The interaction came back to me ten years later, after I had graduated high school, while I was doing a meditation retreat. I was walking through the meditation hall, sunlight streaming through the window onto the wooden floor, when this memory resurfaced, along with the recognition of the radical trust those words and that moment held. I didn't particularly ⬛⬛⬛⬛⬛⬛⬛⬛⬛⬛⬛⬛⬛⬛⬛⬛ weren't offered as a ⬛⬛⬛⬛⬛⬛⬛⬛⬛⬛⬛⬛⬛⬛⬛⬛ nition of something ⬛⬛⬛⬛⬛⬛⬛⬛⬛⬛⬛⬛⬛⬛⬛⬛ Remembering this gesture of trust in my basic humanity, it became so clear how often in my life I had forgotten that trust. It seemed to me then, as tears of sad-joy poured from my eyes, and it still seems to me now that knowing and sharing this trust in the natural goodness of human life is the most important lesson there is.

The prospect of bringing up and educating children in the world today is daunting. When we consider the ecological crises, social injustices, economic disparities, and political conflicts we face, we can't help but feel deeply uneasy, like humanity itself is out of synch with the natural order of things. How do we relate to the feeling this evokes in us? Should we be angry or sad or afraid? Or maybe it's best to simply tune out. Every year I ask my high school students if they think the world overall is progressing or declining. With few exceptions they choose the latter. Given the world they are inheriting, they're not particularly impressed or inspired by the idea that "they are the leaders of the future." "Thanks," they reply, "can't wait…"

And it's not in the future that young people will face challenges. It's now. Today's young people are vulnerable to new dangers, and are experiencing perhaps greater social, emotional, and cultural problems than ever before. Depression, anxiety, distraction, and aggressive behavior are affecting youth at earlier and earlier ages. This is hardly surprising when we look at the forces at play in our culture. We live in an era of information and entertainment saturation, and we're bombarded with constant, paralyzing news about the wrongs of the modern world. Entertainment and meaningless distractions absorb our attention. In real life and in the virtual world, the messages and imagery of violence, hypersexualization, and materialism seep through everywhere.

In every sphere of society, in every kind of activity, we are moving faster than ever before. Our ability to communicate and work efficiently has not yielded greater relaxation, but greater stress. Everyone is busy, and busy is important. No one seems to have *time*. Traditional sources of nourishment, like self-reflection, time in nature, and the ordinary intimacies of living social interaction are often forgotten and devalued. At the deepest and most simple level, many of us feel ill at ease, doubtful of our worthiness, unable to simply feel content, healthy, and good in our lives.

School is a place where the forces of our culture gather and soak into the lives of our youth. Next to home, school is where young people spend the majority of their time. It's where they grow up and are shaped into members of adult society. This shaping comes down to the everyday experience of being in school. As students sit in the classroom, looking at the color of the walls, absorbing the quality of the light in the room, hearing the sounds all around them, they feel and sense their world. They watch each other, learning about relationships and interactions, and discovering how others respond to them when they act in different ways. They feel the pace and rhythms of their days and weeks. And they watch their teachers, feeling and integrating how we relate to them, how we speak and move, how we are as human beings altogether. It has been said that the waters around Atlantis rose so slowly that the people gradually learned to breathe underwater. Just so, young people learn to breathe our culture. As we grow up, our collective values and assumptions about ourselves, society, nature, and reality itself become normal and almost invisible to us.

Education is often heralded as the solution to society's ills. There can be no doubt that learning allows us to raise our consciousness, to overcome ignorance, and to find and apply solutions to our problems both individually and socially. Therefore, as we often hear, we need better education—and more of it. Yet our notion of education is often too narrow, focusing on curriculums and measurable outcomes without acknowledging the deep cultural patterning that it's responsible for.

Our cultural education, this often unquestioned sense of how things are and how we should act and be, affects us profoundly. It is interdependent with how we feel as human beings on a very fundamental level. Until we look into this root feeling, this basic quality of our experience, we have little hope of shifting the direction of our culture, our society, or our world. More and better education will help us learn and may help us address our challenges, but it will always be like trying to cut down a tree by trimming the leaves. If we only train our young people to think and feel the same way previous generations have, how can we expect to get different results, or for our society to change direction?

When asked what students will need to know in the future I've often heard teachers respond that we can't know, but the most important thing is that they learn how to think. This is true, but it may not be enough. Thinking is an incredible capacity, but it's not all we do or all we are. In addition to raising our collective consciousness through traditional thinking and knowledge, we need to *lower* our consciousness and learn to operate not only from our heads. We need to rediscover the wisdom in our bodies, in our hearts, and in our relationships to nature and each other.

A full sense of education means cultivating the whole person. And a person can't be separated from the culture and society they interact with. In this sense, our role as teachers takes on a new dimension. We are in a position to be the architects of a new culture. Thus the onus is on us to be visionary as well as down to earth, to embody as best we can what we hope our students will embody even more fully in the future. In traditional societies it was assumed that young people would benefit from time spent with the elders, the holders of wisdom and tradition. The elders would impart their learning not only through explicit teaching, but also in their way of being in the world. Through hints and by example, in what they did as well as what they did not do, elders would transmit the inner heart of their culture.

I see no reason why teachers can't be the elders, the wisdom holders, for our young people today. Goodness knows our youth need people in their lives who have some depth and vitality as well as patience and compassion. In order for this to become possible, teachers need a way to nourish and strengthen themselves. We need to not only be able to de-stress, but also to discover a deeper wellspring of energy and inspiration from which to operate. Our purpose is not just to do our jobs more effectively, but to engage with the whole endeavor in a transformative way.

My inspiration comes from the principles of the Shambhala meditation path, which have been a guide for me in my teaching career and since my childhood. Shambhala is an ancient tradition that provides a source of learning, culture, and vision that can be applied to all aspects of modern life. It is based on the understanding that we all possess a fundamental wisdom and goodness that can help us overcome our challenges and create a more enlightened world. This is not a spiritual or religious approach, but it is about coming to know a quality of sacredness, or deep worthiness, in our lives and in our teaching. Most of all it is about discovering trust in our own beings, and learning to share that blessing with others.

This book is about fostering our inner life and walking the inner path in the art of teaching. The notion of a path is that we walk one step at a time, moving from habit to heart. Each step is best approached with an attitude of gentle self-reflection, contemplation, and interest in moving forward. This is not a collection of tips or lessons that we can read about today and then go apply to our classroom tomorrow. Rather, it's about how we can bravely work with ourselves as we are and how we can cultivate our innate qualities, allowing them to shine out and illuminate our lives, our teaching, and our world.

Teaching With Bravery is about how we as teachers can nourish ourselves. It is not a book of teaching techniques—it's not even about how to be better teachers in the conventional sense. Rather, it's about cultivating something more fundamental and universal than our pedagogies: a fresh humanity, which can infuse our teaching with new life.

I grew up in the Shambhala tradition and began practicing meditation when I was quite young. When I grew older I became a Shambhala instructor and began leading meditation programs and retreats, which were attended mostly by adults. At the same time, I enjoyed working with young people and went on to become a schoolteacher. After working with the Shambhala principles in the first ten years of my school career, I began leading retreats for schoolteachers. Knowing that teachers work with all ages and in many different systems, I didn't seek to offer many specific suggestions about what to do in the classroom, but instead focused on the discovery of insight arising from our own experience. At first some teachers found this confusing, as they were so accustomed to being introduced to new systems, new curriculums, and new methods. My intention was to peel away the systems, revealing something more essential in how we are as teachers and as human beings altogether. As we will see, simplicity is very sophisticated, and also very important in relating with young people. Pretty quickly, the teachers I worked with began to relax. Then they began to remember something tremendously important, something that perhaps had been missing or obscured in their quest to be effective educators: their hearts. As one teacher remarked, "Usually when I go to a seminar I end up wanting to learn how to be like the person who is leading it. I want to become a teacher like them. But in this case, I've become much more curious about myself—who I am as a teacher, and what kind of teacher I can become."

I was encouraged by fellow teachers, friends, and students to write this book. I hope it will bring guidance and inspiration to educators as well as parents and anyone else who works with young people, who are indeed the leaders of the future, the princes, princesses, and warriors of the present.

Each chapter is a contemplation of an aspect of the brave teacher's journey and is meant to inspire, deepen, or provoke the teacher's innate intelligence. Some chapters include exercises or meditations that you can work with in order to bring the journey into your own experience. You might like to read through the whole book and then go back and work through each chapter, including the exercises, over a period of time. Once you've become familiar with them, you can go back to them as you wish or whenever a certain part feels like the antidote to your current challenge.

Okay, please take a seat. Class is starting.

PART I: TEACHING LIKE A HUMAN BEING

The first step is to simply acknowledge our humanity and the humanity of others. Before we teach and before we learn, we are already complete, worthy, and good. This is a secret that nourishes us, and that we can learn to share.

{ Innocence }

Over lunch three ninth-graders were discussing a hypothetical: If you could live in any time and meet any one person who has ever lived, whom would you choose to meet? Emma answered quickly, "The Buddha." Dave thought a moment, then smiled and said, "Louis Armstrong." William was pensive at first, and then said softly, "I'd like to meet my mother."

Perhaps, like me, you find each of these answers surprising and touching in different ways, and you can probably identify with each of them on some level. We all have a longing to know something profound and compassionate, something creative and beautiful, and above all something authentic in our lives. There is tenderness in this longing. It carries a hint of delight, but also one of sadness. Longing feels like our heart pulling us to reconnect. We yearn to come home to something we have known but do not feel is complete and present in our lives now. If we didn't know it somewhere within us, we wouldn't long for it. We long because we have a heart.

This kind of longing is very different from the wants and cravings that run through our heads on the daily. Our minds constantly generate all kinds of desires for things outside of ourselves. We imagine and project that the next thing—the next cup of coffee, the next lover, the next app, the next affirmation, the next job well done—will be the one that satisfies us, but the wanting goes on and on. It ebbs and flows, but is ultimately insatiable. This wanting is really a proxy for our deeper longing to feel content within our own being. We would like to be at home in our lives.

It's like hearing the echo of our own humanity. Deep down we *know* ourselves to be whole, not broken. We know ourselves to be alive, not numb. Yet somehow, wandering the roads of life, we have become disconnected from something fundamental. Our wish to return to it pulses within us.

In the Shambhala tradition, that fundamental aliveness is known as *basic goodness*. It is the natural, innate wisdom of all people. It's called *basic* goodness because it is the base, the foundation of our experience. In spite of all our confusion, goodness is the undaunted core of our humanity. Teachers often have an intuitive sense of this natural goodness. We can see it manifest in our students in the moments when their light shines through, expressive and unobstructed. In a student's simple, unplanned smile or in a child's spontaneous stroke of yellow paint, we see little hints of their unadorned humanity. When a shy student raises her hand we might see a flash of that simple tenderness just before we call on her.

Our appreciation of those moments reveals our own basic goodness. There is a spark of total joy when we release our personal agenda and open to others. When we hear, see, or touch our world, feeling its textures directly, we find our own heart in a moment. We are reconnecting with the primal openness that is the base of our humanity. It is completely nonconceptual, and cannot be fully described with words. It's also completely ordinary. The simple feeling of life in each moment—the sudden coolness of a glass of ice water on a summer day, the whiteness of a cloud, the swatch of red color we see where the billboard paper is torn away—contains a fullness, a freshness. You can see this experience in the face of a young child when he looks at his world, seeing a flower or a tree, perhaps for the very first time. We may no longer experience the world in that fresh and pure way, yet the capacity is still within us. We could call it the *innocence principle*. Whether we are young or old, it is our nature as human beings.

Needless to say, humanity expresses itself in other ways, too. People are capable of tremendous aggression, degradation, and confusion. Even very young children can be nasty as hell. The notion of basic goodness does not deny that darkness and confusion exist and often dominate our world. Yet even when it is buried deep, forgotten under layers of doubt, fear, aggression, and habit, that innocence remains, pure and fresh. Generally, we miss it because we're accustomed and educated to put our attention elsewhere. As we go through our lives we rarely give ourselves space and time to simply experience things in an unbiased way. We tend to forget that we can just be alive without doing something. We are always thinking about what's going on rather than simply being in it. A fall breeze touches us, and for an almost imperceptible moment we just feel it—how it is cool and warm at the same time, how it carries a hint of wood smoke and a hint of ice. That moment in which we are open, directly in contact with our experience, is basic goodness. But our mental commentary very quickly steps in and overtakes our attention, and we revert back to tasks at hand, or to looping discursive thoughts, or to memories, worries, and pop songs running through our heads. With babbling thoughts and preoccupations we blanket ourselves against the raw, direct openness of our experience. Having gotten used to this blanket, we can hardly imagine life without it. Yet it blocks out the magic of our lives. We no longer really see the cloud or the flower. We regard them as unimportant. Dwelling in thoughts of past and future, the experience of life itself, in this very moment, eludes us.

At the root of this habit is a fear that we are not good, that we are not worthy just as we are. We are afraid to rest because we don't know how to be with ourselves. There is an underlying insecurity that haunts us like a little gremlin who whispers and whines in our ear about how we look funny, how we're out of shape, lazy, dumb, inadequate. Sometimes we fight the gremlin by trying to prove it wrong. Other times we try to drown out its voice by filling our lives with distraction, keeping our bodies busy, and fixing our mental energy on little personal dramas. But our efforts to ignore the gremlin's voice only feed it and make it stronger. This might sound dramatic, but we experience it as everyday life, business as usual. Over time the struggle burns us out, leaving us exhausted, jaded, and uninspired.

The gremlin is really just a little habit that lives in us, a flicker of doubt about our worthiness. But its voice gets amplified in our culture. Our little doubts are nurtured by our upbringing, in the images we see in movies and magazines, in how we measure social status by money, sex, and credentials. Our collective sense of self forms the basis of our culture, which in turn shapes the way that we feel about ourselves.

These deep social themes also play themselves out in the cultures of our schools. In school, like in a greenhouse, the elements of the eco-system are magnified, and their effects on the seedlings are increased. Sadly, school culture too often fosters a sense of unworthiness. In many schools the environment almost proclaims it with the gloomy, institutional feeling of the buildings, the painted concrete, the scarcity of natural light, the jarring buzzers, and the crashing of metal lockers. The social environment feels both severe and childish, reflecting an absence of mutual respect between teachers and students. The learning environment is boring and lifeless yet somehow threatening as well. The dangers of failure and shame are always looming. Students are measured and assessed based on static objectives and competition. Learning, which begins as a natural process, becomes a heavy burden. Students develop a vague sense that school is a process of enduring someone else's agenda, and for many, day-to-day school life is dull, lonesome, and dreadful.

The principle of basic goodness provides a ground of possibility for transforming this culture of fear. While no one can solve all the difficult issues at play, our own mind and our own basic outlook on life provide a powerful starting place. In the Shambhala teachings it is said that the "mind of fearfulness should be put in the cradle of loving-kindness."[1] The fearful mind is one that has lost its ability to be with itself. It has lost trust in itself. We all have this fearful mind—not just children. Fear is the cause of our confusion, selfishness, greed, and jealousy. Our collective fearful mind generates a greater culture of materialism and aggression. Placing that fearful mind in the cradle of loving-kindness does not mean indulging it. Rather, it means giving the mind space and nourishment so that it can relax and settle back into its natural, open state.

Chögyam Trungpa, the founder of the Shambhala tradition, wrote a treatise on how to educate a prince or princess—someone who would grow up to be a brave, compassionate, skillful, and joyous leader. The treatise states that the prince's education should occur in an environment free of jealousy and competition, and that those who raise the prince should not think in terms of raising a child in the conventional sense. Rather, they should take the attitude that they are educating the sky. Then the prince will begin to have inquisitiveness toward the world, developing wonder about the details and processes of things. The image of educating the sky is a poetic gesture toward the principle of trust in human nature. Rather than seeing ourselves, or our students, as stupid to begin with but with potential to become educated, we regard the human being as fundamentally whole. Educating as though we were teaching the sky means working with students in a way that supports and encourages their innate wisdom, rather than guiding them away from it.

The vision of basic goodness represents a profound shift. It prioritizes humanity ahead of outcomes, policies, money, or theory. Recently my friend Nikki told me a story of her experience as a nurse. She does home-care with children who are dependent on life-sustaining apparatuses and who can't communicate. Nikki said it was clear to her that although the children were unresponsive, they were aware. She began to practice speaking to them and relating to them directly. It felt essential to her to put their humanity first. Many of the other nurses, she said, assumed the children were unaware, and would only relate to the machines—checking their settings, making adjustments, and then checking their smartphones before leaving. The response of the parents to Nikki's way of being with their children was dramatic. They called her an angel, and felt incredible gratitude to her for honoring their children as human beings. Before we are teachers, we are human beings. Before we are students or parents, successes or failures, we are human beings. Simple as this truth may be, the symptoms in our culture indicate that as a society we've lost track of something essential. We have underestimated and downgraded what it means to be human. Now is the time to restore humanity to the center of our lives and our culture.

Rather than beginning from the perspective of a problem to be remedied, we can take a brave leap into the view that human beings are fundamentally good. Each child possesses a mind and a heart that is brilliant like the sun, deep like the ocean, and delicate like a drop of rain. We all have challenges and shortcomings, but our basic being is unblemished. Young people naturally lack perspective, experience, and knowledge. They also suffer from the confusion of growing up and experiencing unkindness in their lives. Knowing the essential goodness of our students allows us to honor their experience in its full context. Then education can be a process in which our inner humanity blossoms, rather than one in which it is gradually forgotten.

1st Assignment:

Contemplate basic goodness.
Think of an experience that touched your heart. Recall a moment when you saw the world with fresh eyes and felt wonder, like a child in a flower garden. Think of a time when someone, maybe a student in your class, expressed their humanity in a way that was so raw and true that it brought you back to your heart.

{ An Inner Path }

Teaching is a challenging occupation in most cases and perhaps impossible in some. Many teachers work in conditions that restrict their chances of breathing life into their classrooms. Whether this is your situation or whether you teach in an idyllic, free, and creative environment, we all have a common basis, which is our human experience. In order to relate with others, to care for and teach our students in a genuine way, we have to begin with ourselves. Teaching involves giving a tremendous amount of ourselves and absorbing a tremendous amount from our students. Every day in my classroom I make countless decisions, I surf the wave of changing circumstances, I make progress and I make mistakes. It can be exhausting and exhilarating, all in one class period. Teachers are under a lot of pressure to do a good job, often under conditions that obstruct their chances of success. With all of this, it's natural that we tend to be pragmatic and professionally minded, always on the lookout for ways to make our teaching more effective and more efficient. But if we genuinely wish to discover a deeper way of being as teachers and as human beings, we need to slow down. Our professional development is essential to our teaching craft, but it should begin with a process of personal reflection. Otherwise, while we may become effective educators on one level, what we communicate implicitly to others will be dictated by the habitual patterns that simmer beneath our awareness. Themes of self-loathing, stress, and judgment seep into the classroom like tea infusing hot water. This doesn't serve our youth well. As education luminary Parker Palmer said, "If for some reason you choose to live an unexamined life... I beg of you, do not take a job that involves other people."[2]

There is an inner path of teaching, as well as an outer path. The outer path is about our work as teachers, our methods, lessons, plans, and techniques, which we constantly refine and develop throughout our careers. The inner path is the journey of our personal feelings and reflections. It's about how we experience and understand ourselves, our students, and the process of teaching. Our inner journey informs and shapes the outcomes of our work in ways that are not as easy to measure, but are nevertheless dramatic and often easy to feel. Having a vital inner life can imbue our work and the culture of our classrooms with meaning. When we discover an inner sense of wealth, it's not difficult to find ways to offer and share it. On the other hand, if the foundation of our inner life is a deep-seated sense of inadequacy, all of our efforts and techniques will feel like attempts to compensate for that underlying wound.

If you think about Chögyam Trungpa's image of educating the sky, it might occur to you that it's impossible. We can't teach the sky! On the other hand, we can teach in a way that helps young people know their own hearts and minds, which are limitless, luminous, and good. Just saying so won't do much. To make it meaningful, we have to embody it. We need to know it as genuine experience, not just theory. Fortunately, we have all we need to make this real. We are human beings ourselves, so we have an inherently workable basis.

Study Hall:

Consider your inner life as a teacher. How do you feel when you go to school? Do you have a sense of vitality, meaning, curiosity, learning? Or are there feelings of dread, heaviness, resignation? Be gentle—there's no praise or blame, just have a look with honest curiosity.

{ Trust }

Our deepest habitual pattern is our inability to simply *be*. Whether we are by ourselves or with others, we have become deeply accustomed to feeling that we need to change how we are. We feel that we are somehow incomplete. We can see the symptoms of this habit in our everyday life. There is a feeling of restlessness and a desire for constant preoccupation that runs through our days. We have a difficult time relating to gaps in the program of our day—waiting for the bus, standing in line, even downloading a file. With nothing but ourselves to fill the space we get antsy. We are uncomfortable with ourselves at a deep level and feel that somehow our experience isn't what it should be. Our culture encourages this habit, giving us endless ways to divert our attention. Consumerism constantly gnaws at us, reminding us of things we want, suggesting that we are imperfect as we are, but that we could be alright if we bought some styling mousse, or a new device, or a pizza, or maybe if we started going to yoga classes, got some professional coaching, or found love. The theme of "not good as you are" also runs through our educational culture with its emphasis on evaluation and its use of shame and fear for motivation.

Out of this pervasive feeling of uneasiness comes a sense of separation. We feel separate from ourselves to begin with—we're uneasy with our own experiences, emotions, and thoughts. We constantly struggle with ourselves, trying to escape discomfort and uncertainty. We are always avoiding ourselves, and our anxiety generates a lot of mental speed. Our thoughts race and wander from one fixation to the next. We would like to get away from the stress in our lives, but we rarely reflect on where it comes from. We are constantly assessing our experiences in relation to whether we like or dislike them. Because we don't trust ourselves at a basic level, we feel the need to constantly fret over our persona, seeking reassurances that we are valid. Yet this project never stops. Even a simple experience like walking into a room and being unsure of where to sit can be enough to make us question our whole existence.

The principle of basic goodness is that it is possible to trust ourselves. Trust here does not simply mean having some kind of faith that things will work out, that we will somehow make the right decision in every situation, or that we can rely on our credentials. Rather, it means being open to our life as it is. Each experience, whether hot or cold, painful or pleasurable, funny or tragic, is an expression of basic goodness, basic humanity.

A few years ago, "It's all good" was a popular expression among teenagers. It could seemingly be applied to any situation—in response to "John, you haven't handed in the last five assignments," John could say, "It's all good!" which could be roughly translated, "I prefer not to relate with that today!" This kind of cheerful ignorance is quite different from basic goodness. Every situation is not good in the sense that it will work out well or that it has a silver lining. Our actual experience in life, and certainly in our classrooms, has its ups and downs. Sometimes things come together beautifully—we walk into our classroom and our students are spontaneously reciting Shakespeare and we think, "Ah… my work here is done!" Other times our classes are abysmal. We come in and students are shouting, crying, and throwing things, or everyone is half asleep, no one has done the reading or even brought the book to class. We feel disgusted and angry.

But whatever we feel, we can't reject the situation completely because we always have basic goodness. Knowing this, inwardly we can relax a little. We can subtly shift toward being open and inquisitive. Each moment of our life is worthy of our full attention. When we feel bad, or when we feel good, the first part is that we *feel*. That's where the wisdom is. If we are willing to feel what we feel, see what we see, hear what we hear—rather than struggling against our experience—we can come back to ourselves. We can see the reality and potential in each moment of our life. It may feel raw, edgy, exposed, emotional, or confusing, but it is where we are, and it is worthy and good.

Despite our ups and downs, there is something within us that is solid, like good earth. When we feel the earth it is so rich, so wholesome. We can smell the soil and moss and pine needles. We can feel the depth and solidity of the earth. It is trustworthy. It is not fundamentally impoverished. We can discover this worthy sense of being within ourselves. When we feel it, we can relax. We can afford to trust that we are in the right place.

The everyday practice of trust is to simply feel and touch our experience in the moment. Rather than surveying and analyzing our lives from our heads, we can experience our lives with our whole being. Bringing our awareness *down* into our bodies, we can invoke our intuitive awareness. We feel what we feel, see what we see, hear what we hear, and smell what we smell.

You could do this right now, while you're reading. For a minute, just feel. Allow your center of gravity to drop down from your head into your whole body. Make a subtle shift toward being inquisitive and open to what you are feeling and perceiving. Feel the quality of your inner weather—the textures and qualities of your emotional state. Feel the temperature of the air. Feel your feet and the center of your body.

This practice of feeling and trusting boycotts our habit of wanting to be other than we are, which is a strong habit. For example, if we have to teach on a morning when we haven't slept well and we're presenting a lesson that we are a bit unsure about, we will probably be experiencing a rich brew of feelings. Maybe we drank more coffee than necessary, so we feel a bit wired. There is a slight quivering in our chest and our hands are shaky. We're not sure how to begin and our students can sense our hesitation. This is not an extreme or unusual scenario (at least not for me), but it is one that has a bit of an edge to it. We would rather feel settled, rested, and confident, so we feel critical of ourselves and eager to get through the morning. If we seize upon our thinking process alone, we might start burying ourselves under an avalanche of self-criticism, or we might just switch into default mode: get by, numb out, wait for the end of the day.

At any moment in the midst of this we can decide to trust. We can simply decide to commit to ourselves and be with our current experience. We can come into our sense perceptions, into our bodies, and feel our experience as it is right now. Our hands are a little shaky, so we feel that. We don't have to pile commentary on top of it. We have a feeling of edginess, so we just feel that. We stay with ourselves, and with the whole thing. We don't have to alter or control what arises. We trust—we decide that being human is good.

Tutorial:

Sit quietly for two minutes and just feel your experience as it is right now. Whatever you feel, hear, or perceive in your body and mind, simply regard it as the expression of your humanity. It is worthy and natural. This is trust.

Care

Part of the challenge is that we are ridiculously harsh with ourselves. We criticize ourselves for being too busy when we feel stressed out, and for being lazy when we relax. We judge our bodies, our faces, our hair, and the sound of our own voice. We love finding ways to feel bad about ourselves and we're very creative about it. Even if we don't focus the feeling on something specific, we're haunted by a vague sense of "doing it wrong."

For me, one of my biggest challenges in teaching is a lingering feeling of inadequacy. Every student needs more help, more attention, more challenges perfectly crafted to his or her or their needs. Every lesson could be improved. I need more training and professional development. I need to learn more about my subjects. Besides that, we are not only called upon to be scholars. We're needed as psychologists, disciplinarians, therapists, family counselors, cheerleaders, playmates, social workers, mediators, janitors, administrators, fundraisers, bouncers, cultural awareness experts… wilderness guides… gardeners… what else? It's not reasonable to think we could meet all these expectations of course, but we still feel their pull. Any one of them could be a full-time occupation. This longing to help can be a positive attribute, and one that motivates us to be excellent in our jobs. But it can also feed into our sense of self-criticism. It's easy to get trapped in a cycle of inadequacy and defensiveness, leaving us brittle and burned out.

Again, our inner world is interdependent with society at large, and this sense of self-loathing is a habit ingrained in our cultural body. Education is all too often a process of gradually breaking down a child's sense of self-worth. While success in school is praised, celebrated, and even rewarded with prizes, lagging students are often intentionally made to feel miserable and embarrassed. I recently read about a school in which a teacher was criticized by the assistant principal for not thoroughly castigating a student who had a wrong answer on a paper.[3] The teacher was told that she should have ripped the student's paper up in front of her. This may be an extreme example, but it's common for schools to promote a culture of *conditionality*. We learn that we can earn acceptance and praise, and in the future supposedly we can earn money and thus happiness, *if* we do well in school. But even if we play this game well and succeed in both school and adult life, we may find happiness elusive. We simply haven't developed the capacity for it. Instead we've layered in the habit of unhappiness.

We have so many ideas about how we should be perfect, about how we should feel, act, and look. And we use these ideas to steer ourselves away from how we actually feel. In order to unravel our addiction to self-loathing, we need to foster a sense of unconditional care for ourselves as we are. With trust we can open ourselves to feeling whatever is arising. Care is handling that experience with loving-kindness.

Genuine care is not developed as an overlay onto our experience, like affirmations or positive thinking. Rather, it's a practice of softening. Have you ever been in an argument with someone and suddenly realized that what they're saying is totally reasonable? At that point, we could puff up our pride and keep arguing, but usually we let down our guard and breathe a sigh of relief. That's what softening feels like. Whatever arises, we can be soft and curious, at least inwardly. When we find ourselves freezing up with habitual reactions, we can let ourselves melt. We have been so alienated from ourselves that many of us are completely out of touch with what we actually feel, let alone see, and hear, and so on. Practicing care means taking an interest in meeting ourselves anew. We are taking an attitude of friendship with ourselves, which is not about pampering ourselves with pleasure. A good friend listens with warmth and inquisitiveness. Thus we listen to our own experience. We might be tasting a strawberry, or we might have a pain in our shoulder. We can "listen" to what is happening in an open way, as we would with a good friend. Care is being gentle as well as present. It is a practice of healing.

It takes intention to develop friendship with ourselves. We're creating a new culture in the country of our own mind, which has been a war zone for a long time. Gangs of habitual patterns have been running the show, and they won't surrender their knives immediately. They're also clever—even our efforts to develop self-kindness through activities like meditation, resting, or walking in the garden can be co-opted by the gangsters into forms of self-criticism. So we need to bring a steady intention, a sort of gentle stubbornness, to our effort.

We can observe the tone of voice that we use with ourselves in our heads. If we notice that we're speaking in a harsh way, we can soften our tone. Many of us speak to ourselves as if we were our own worst enemy, cursing ourselves for little mistakes like dropping our keys. We could give ourselves a break. That break may only last a moment before we plunge back into habit, but in each moment we are planting the seeds of a new outlook.

The main practice is just to start over each time we notice the edge of harshness coming up. Even if we are feeling really bad and we've made some real mistakes, we can take a fresh start and soften into the feelings that are arising. If we don't like how we feel, we have an opportunity to practice gentleness. That is the moment to soften, to generate a sense of care, warmth, and curiosity toward how we actually feel. What we are feeling is our humanity. It's not always comfortable; it can be raw, vivid, scary, and uncertain. Yet remaining gentle in these moments is how we begin to shift our allegiance away from habits of distraction, blame, and depression.

The process of befriending ourselves begins as a radical move. Just like the culture of a society, our inner culture is a set of norms— ways of being and interacting that are so ingrained they become invisible to us from the inside. When something goes against the norm, it stands out. It looks and feels awkward. Yet over time a society's values and ways of being can shift to a new normal. Gradually the culture of our inner life can become more kind. When we begin to gain familiarity with ourselves we find that this sense of care is natural. We don't have to pretend to feel warmth and curiosity about our lives. Care is an aspect of our basic goodness. We just have to remember to stop stopping it. Kindness wants to blossom. The practice is allowing it to blossom.

Tutorial:

Sit quietly for a few minutes. Let your attention sink down into your whole body. Allow yourself to feel whatever is currently arising.

Now, tune into the natural undercurrent of care. However you feel and whatever you see, hear, etc., notice that you have an underlying curiosity and tenderness toward your experience.

As you feel sensations and perceive your world, soften.

Accept yourself with warmth and space.

Homework:

Between now and tomorrow, notice how you talk to yourself in your head. Notice the attitude and the tone of voice you bring to your inner life as you go about your daily activity. If you notice harshness, just start fresh and soften.

True Relaxation

The fruition of developing trust and care for ourselves is realizing that we can let go. We are able to recognize the self-existing nature of basic goodness. What that means is that we don't have to build and maintain our persona all the time. We could actually drop the whole project of "me." We could just relax. Basic goodness, who we truly are, is there already. We don't have to keep squirming, thinking, stressing, and spinning the record in order to maintain ourselves. Relaxing would not cause us to die on the spot, to lose ourselves, or to forget what we are doing.

We naturally let go at various times in our lives, sort of by accident—when hearing a beautiful piece of music, or standing at the edge of the ocean, or falling in love, for example. For a little while we feel as though we lose ourselves in something bigger. In those moments we feel full and alive. We lose track of our agenda for how we should be feeling, and we open up. With less self-fixation drawing us down into our own whirlpool, our attention and awareness can relax and expand out.

Letting go is not what we're used to, though, and it may sound like the opposite of relaxing. If you think about dropping your armor, letting go of yourself, how do you feel?

{ Vulnerability }

Another core aspect of being human is the feeling of vulnerability. Even if we are super-soldiers or arch-villains, we are never completely beastly, covered over with aggression—tooth, fang, and nail against the world. We have a soft spot, a tender and open part of ourselves. That tenderness allows us to take in and be touched by life. If we see blackberries ripening and we pick some and eat them, we are being vulnerable, showing our softness and connection to our world. To be alive we need to be receptive and open. Our senses are soft and yielding, allowing us to see, hear, taste, smell, and feel. As much as this is an integral aspect of life, and as much as we don't actually want to be numb or closed off, for most of us this quality of vulnerability is a source of constant struggle and uneasiness.

Conventionally, being vulnerable means being susceptible to harm. While we want to taste the blackberry, we know that reaching for it makes us vulnerable to the thorns. In that sense, simply not wanting to be harmed is a natural and intelligent reflex. When we talk about acknowledging our vulnerability, we are not saying we should open ourselves up to harm in a naïve way. As teachers we often have to be tough. We need the qualities of resilience, authority, and sometimes fierceness. We are also not saying we have to share excessively and expose our shortcomings, revealing the weak spots in our résumés, sharing all of our tender feelings, and so on. This kind of behavior may or may not be skillful in any given situation.

Here, acknowledging vulnerability means being willing to experience life without covering over, explaining away, or hiding. Vulnerability is allowing life's vivid, colorful chaos to touch our awareness and to touch our hearts. It means actually tasting the blackberry, or actually feeling the thorns scratch us. When we are open to our vulnerability, we experience things fully and directly. Life touches us with its fragility, sadness, and exquisite fullness. Again, we don't have to make this happen. As human beings, we are designed to let life in. It just pours in, like an ocean, in every moment.

While we long to feel alive and connected, we often don't know how to handle the rawness and exposure that it brings. A soft, inquisitive, and tender impulse is constantly emerging in us, but we usually work to cover it over. We've learned to feel that vulnerability is weakness. In our movies, ways of conversing, and social habits we glorify aggression over gentleness, control over openness, men over women, armies over schools. We're taught not to show the soft side of ourselves: our tears, our uncertainty, our tenderness. We craft our personalities carefully to protect us from appearing vulnerable. We fill the space of our lives with busyness, noise, and entertainment in order to avoid meeting ourselves in that raw and exposed place.

Feeling touched by life brings a feeling of uncertainty, which often evokes fear. Fear tends to provoke more fear—a sense of panic, which then makes us want to armor up. For example, if we are meeting some parents to discuss a difficulty with their child, we don't know how they will respond, so we feel some uncertainty. Our uncertainty, as well as our connection and care for the child, makes us feel vulnerable, which evokes fear. We attempt to quash our fear and put on our professional armor, presenting our case to the parents as a matter of fact. This causes the parents to feel shamed, so they respond with fear, possibly becoming angry at us, or more likely, at their child.

If we reverse engineer this scenario, peeling back the anger, the armor, the fear on top of fear, we come back to tenderness. That tenderness, or vulnerability, is the gateway to life and growth. Everyone has this softness, but few have developed the trust and care needed to be at ease with it. Real strength comes from learning to feel it, learning to trust. If we meet those parents with our hearts open, even as we feel our fear and uncertainty, we create a space that their hearts can open into, and a genuine meeting of minds becomes possible around our shared concern for the child.

> Rachael Kessler, author of *The Soul of Education*, writes,
>
> A teacher with an open heart can be warm, alive, spontaneous, connected, compassionate. He or she can see the language of the body and hear the feelings between the words. An open heart is what allows a teacher to be trustworthy and to help build trust among his or her students. To have an open heart, a teacher must be willing to be vulnerable and willing to care…To be vulnerable is to be willing to feel deeply, to be moved by what a student expresses

or by what comes up inside ourselves in the presence
of our students or the issues they raise.[4]

We might think we have to choose between vulnerability and
confidence, but this is a false dynamic. As we practice being soft
and vulnerable we begin to feel more at ease with ourselves. Our
fear and uncertainty no longer terrify us, and therefore we feel more
appreciation, spontaneity, and humor. For example, my friend Norah
teaches very young children. One day she called a class meeting to
discuss her concern that too many children were calling each other
"poop head." She opened the meeting by explaining that this name
wasn't very nice, but that she understood that name-calling happens,
so maybe the class could come up with some names that would be
more appropriate. Right away a little boy raised his hand and said,
"How about motherfucker?"

The surprise and humor in that story are a bit obvious. Most
of the time appreciation doesn't have a punch line, but we can find
delight in ordinary life. As Chögyam Trungpa wrote, "We should
feel that it is wonderful to be in this world. How wonderful it is to
see red and yellow, blue and green, purple and black! All of these
colors are provided for us. We feel hot and cold; we taste sweet
and sour. We have these sensations and we deserve them. They are
good."[5]

When we let down our guard we feel a more intimate connection
with life. We are dissolving the boundaries that separate us from the
world. With this vulnerability and softness we may feel a bit lonely,
but there is also a sense of wholesomeness and healthiness in allowing
ourselves to be human, as we are.

Tutorial:

Give yourself five minutes to just feel what it is to be human.

- ❖ Trust that what you are currently experiencing is an expression of your humanity, which is worthy and good. Let your attention drop into your whole body and feel what is happening in your current experience.
- ❖ As you feel and perceive what is arising, have a caring and gentle attitude toward yourself.
- ❖ Acknowledge your vulnerability, allowing yourself to be touched by the unique colors, sounds, textures, and energies of life.

Recess:

Go for a walk or have a cup of tea. Are these simple human qualities still there when you're not trying to foster them?

{ Being Human in the Classroom }

Recently my friend Toby told me about getting his fifth-grade report card. Toby was doing poorly in almost all of his classes, and his report cited almost across the board disruptive and disrespectful behavior. The exception was Choir, in which Toby was described as a model student. Naturally, his mother asked him why this was. Toby replied, "Because, Mom, Choir is serious." What did he mean by serious? Grown up Toby explains, "The teacher was real. He was a real person. He cared. I didn't specifically care about Choir, but I had to show up for this teacher."

For most young people, living examples of genuine humanity are few and far between. The majority of adults in their lives have never learned to be with themselves, and are therefore not able to be "real." I often think of Mr. Dane, in whose classroom I volunteered for a time. Mr. Dane handled classes of over forty middle school students with impressive competence. With great intensity and swift discipline, he kept the class in step through each class period. His presence made things clear. It said, "This is the line. Stay on the good side of the line and I'll leave you be." With lots of glaring and shouting, he put the lid on each little outburst of steam. After class Mr. Dane would often swear and kick the chairs. He would refer to students as "complete idiots." When I asked if he liked teaching, he said, "Sometimes, but I'm pretty tired." Strictly speaking, Mr. Dane was good at his job: He delivered curriculum and managed his class under challenging circumstances. But what his students experienced each day was a man whose energy was drawn from anger and frustration.

Children and young people are deeply affected by their environments and the authority figures in their lives. And they suffer, as we all do, from self-doubt and feelings of fear about their inherent worthiness. From the example of their teachers, they draw essential information about how to work with these feelings. Teaching and learning is a dialogue, much of which takes place at different levels of our awareness. Beneath our words and actions, the deepest and most fundamental conversation that takes place is about our basic existence. In his or her heart, each student is asking, "How shall I be?" Our response to that question is demonstrated through our way of being. How we are is something our students feel. It teaches them about humanness. Therefore, to the extent that we can embody a feeling of confidence in the worthiness of being human, that feeling will diffuse to our students.

A story of the Zen poet Ryōkan exemplifies this kind of intuitive human transmission. Ryōkan was a hermit and monk who wandered through the country and villages of Japan. When Ryōkan would come to town, it was said, it was as though spring had arrived. He loved to spend time with children, and his poetry expressed a simple yet profound joy in life. Once Ryōkan was invited to dinner by the parents of a teenage boy who was developing an angry and rebellious disposition. The parents hoped the monk would impart some words of wisdom to the boy and maybe set him straight. The evening progressed, but the parents were disappointed, as Ryōkan said not a word to the lad. As Ryōkan prepared to depart, the boy bent to assist the honored guest with his sandals. Tying on a sandal, the boy felt a drop of moisture on the back of his neck. Looking up he saw the face of Ryōkan gazing down at him, smiling slightly, his eyes wet with tears. After this, though the monk had said nothing to him, the boy's attitude shifted.[6]

Like Ryōkan, we could be genuine and gentle with our students. Naturally, we can encourage them, but we don't have to assault them with our authority or overwhelm them with advice. In the Shambhala fashion, we surround the fearful mind with loving-kindness. Then that fearful mind begins to relax and enjoy the vulnerability and intelligence of an open mind. Without that openness, it is much more difficult to learn. Learning means moving toward the unknown, the uncertain. It means constantly touching the edge of our ignorance. The feeling of not knowing is tender and quivering. From within fear's perspective, it's as if we are standing on a cliff on the shore of the ocean, with the cosmic, dark sky above. In order to learn, we have to step off the edge. As teachers it is our role to guide our students to that edge, but then what? Should we threaten and shame them until they jump? Or maybe bribe them? Those approaches sometimes work to get kids through school, but they rarely awaken a true learning spirit. Gentleness is the expression of trust. We can trust that beneath the layers of fearful mind there is a natural wish to learn. As human beings, we long to know and understand our heritage—the sky, the earth, the animals, the molecules, our stories, the stars, and all the elements of our lives. That spirit, childlike and inquisitive, wants to come out. In a gentle, trusting environment, it will come out.

Gentleness may sound wimpy or touchy-feely, but when it comes to real gentleness, not just pretense, it's not. Real gentleness arises in the absence of fearful aggression. It is the expression of a mind that is not at war with itself. When we feel a sense of wellbeing within ourselves, we don't feel threatened by others. Therefore, with gentleness, we can be as soft or as tough as the situation calls for and the overall environment will still feel infused with trust and kindness. On the other hand, if we are inwardly fearful and conflicted our students will feel our aggression coming through no matter how sweet we try to be.

Gentleness creates a space in which fear and neuroses can begin to play themselves out. Eventually, deprived of the fuel of resistance, they run out of steam. M.K. Asante writes about an experience of this in his amazing memoir *Buck*. "Fuck school," he wrote in his journal on his first day at his new school. "Ok," replied his teacher, laughing, "Now keep writing. Keep going."[7] This response was so completely unexpected—so trusting, so unconcerned about his attitude—that he suddenly didn't know what to do. Looking at the blank page he became curious about what else there was to say. It was a turning point for him, and the beginning of a great love of writing.

The classroom—or wherever we teach[8]—is a *dojo*, a training ground that brings constant challenges. Over and over it knocks us off balance or gives us the opportunity to dance. Developing our inner qualities allows us a place to return to and arise from, a genuine home ground within our own being. By developing trust and care for ourselves, and relaxation with our vulnerability, we are able to be true and genuine human beings and, in turn, teachers. Our students' needs are many. We may not have any idea how to help them, but we can meet them as real people. It's a good place to start.

Test:

Paradoxically, just being ourselves requires deep work and commitment. We are learning to transform ourselves, to be genuine with our students, and ultimately to re-pattern society. Teaching was never for the faint of heart, but this thickens the soup. Therefore, we need to ask ourselves:

- ❖ Am I interested in being human in the classroom?
- ❖ Am I willing to work with myself in an ongoing way, to recognize my fears and habits, and to develop trust, care, and vulnerability?
- ❖ What obstacles or hesitations arise when I contemplate committing myself to this journey?

PART II: TEACHING LIKE A MOUNTAIN

A great teacher is like a mountain. In spite of the wind and rain, the mountain remains steady. When we get lost, the mountain provides a reference point. It continually offers what is of its nature—peace, beauty, and dignity.

{ Sitting Down }

"Sometimes I sit and think, and sometimes I just sit."
—Courtney Barnett

For many teachers, overwhelm is the bread and water of daily life. It's not only the piles of papers to grade or the overall work that can leave us feeling spent at the end of the day. It's also the feeling of being scattered and pulled between many different demands for our attention. You begin to explain an assignment and to write its due date on the board, stop to ask Sammy to open her agenda, continue with the lesson, ask students to open their books, respond to students who forgot to bring theirs to class, begin to discuss the theme of the chapter, notice that Max's shoes are full of holes, see the admin assistant tapping at the door and stop to speak with her about attendance, move to stand beside Gavin so he will settle down, go over the theme again with those who came back from getting their books, locate the missing attendance notebook, note that Ellie is not working and remember that her father just left for an eight-month work trip, and then you're onto the next ten minutes. We are constantly managing an emergent balance of chaos and order, making decisions and judgment calls, responding to dramas ranging from a child's stolen pencil to full-on assaults on our character by parents, students, or coworkers. It's not an easy line of work. It demands a balance of flexibility and resilience, humor and toughness.

Unfortunately, what we often bring to the challenge of teaching is not balance or flexibility, but a brittle mind full of habitual patterns—buzzing thoughts, neurotic fixations, emotional reactivity. Better teaching methods and organizational skills can help us prioritize and function more effectively, but if we want to find a deeper sense of meaning and authenticity in our teaching life we need a way of working with our state of mind. We need a way to bring out the wisdom of goodness in the midst of our busy days, in the midst of our work. The best—and also the simplest—practice for this is meditation.

Although meditation is thousands of years old, it is still relatively new in the Western world and thus fraught with misperceptions. There are also many kinds of meditation, some from ancient sources and some more recent inventions. Not all of these are the same in either method or purpose. In the Shambhala tradition, meditation practice is a simple, secular way of learning to work with our bodies and minds. It's about trusting ourselves and discovering who we are on a very basic level. Meditation develops our positive inner qualities, such as mindfulness, peace, and awareness. It also allows us to recognize and shed our unhelpful habitual patterns such as fear, speedy mind, and aggression. It has many proven benefits, including increased attention, health, and calm. But at its heart, meditation is a simple practice of being fully and straightforwardly human.

The practice consists of sitting still for a period of time, either cross-legged on a cushion or on a chair with our feet on the floor.

We sit in an upright but relaxed manner, breathing naturally. When our attention wanders off, we bring it back to the present. That's pretty much it! So there's not much mystery or belief involved. It's not about going into altered states of consciousness or retreating to a more spiritual place. It's really about becoming familiar with ourselves as we are by just being here, being where we are, and learning to rest in that.

As easy as that may sound, it takes great courage to practice meditation. In many ways, it goes against the grain of everything happening around us. In a speedy, productivity-driven world, meditation stops. In a needy, consumerist world, meditation chills. In a complicated world, meditation just is. In a world of depression and anxiety, meditation proclaims our inherent worthiness. When we sit down to meditate we discover that the currents of confusion that dominate society also flow through our minds. We discover that we are addicted to distraction because we fear the experience of being with ourselves. Sitting down in meditation is a great step toward developing friendship and trust in ourselves. We may not enjoy everything that arises in our minds, but being with it and working with it rather than perpetually running away is a true step toward reclaiming the fullness of life.

Sitting meditation is not only about relieving stress and gaining more peace for ourselves. It also trains us to engage in the world with equanimity. We begin by developing a friendly relationship with our own minds and gradually learn to extend that sense of trust and care to others. When we sit we take the posture of a mountain. Sitting naturally, palms down on our thighs, eyes open, we rest with dignity and strength. We are planted on the earth, solid and powerful, with a sense of openness and acceptance of the sky above and the weather all around. As we sit, many thoughts and emotions come up. We don't follow them or push them out. We allow them to arise, dwell, and naturally disappear. By learning to be with our own energies, feelings, and thoughts, we develop the ability to be with the energy and expression of others. We learn to be the mountain—not ignoring the thunderstorms, rivers, sunshine, snow, and trees, but also not being overwhelmed by them. For our students this means we can be immovable but accommodating, gentle but awesome.

Quiet Corner:

Take some time to consider where you can practice meditation. As we know, students who have a good place to study have an easier time getting around to studying. Just so, it's very supportive to have a place where you can practice being with yourself quietly, without distractions. Set up a small area of your room or somewhere in your home where you can keep a meditation cushion or chair. An uplifted spot with good light is best, but any simple space will work. Clear the space of distractions and clutter. Make it simple and inviting. Also consider whether there are places at work where you could sit quietly at times. For example, during prep periods I occasionally just swivel my office chair away from my desk and spend a few minutes sitting facing the window.

Being Still

Bugaku is a traditional dance of the imperial court of Japan. It is stately, ceremonial, precise, and theatrical, and when you watch bugaku being performed, what is most surprising is the stillness that seems to hold and surround the movements of the dance. The dancers often come to a complete stop, holding a pose with a heightened sense of sublime, relaxed intensity. Because of this stillness, each movement is clear, definite, and striking. A dancer may simply take a step or open a fan, but that gesture is executed with a quality of almost mythical import and confidence. It's totally epic, as my students might say. Witnessing this dance can give us a sense of how stillness can be the basic background for action—how stillness can be dynamic while action can be peaceful. This kind of stillness is the foundation of meditation practice.

For many of us who are very busy, stillness—essentially doing nothing—might seem like a waste of time. But learning to appreciate stillness can bring newfound clarity and elegance to our actions. Rather than running our lives on the fuel of stress and coffee, and regenerating only when we get exhausted or sick, we can utilize stillness to bring a sense of ease and energy to our everyday life.

There's certainly nothing wrong with being busy, but for many of us our activity lacks balance. Our lives have little space; we are *always* doing something. Even when we relax we fill our time with activity and we validate our relaxation as being in the service of future productivity. We have trouble just doing one thing, so we multitask. We turn on the radio while we cook or pop in our earbuds on the bus. We check our email from our phones while we stand in line at the supermarket, and if the line is slow, we might even get a little work done. In our minds, we think and think and think, filling the inner space as much as we fill the outer space. We're always in a hurry. Being such busybodies, it's difficult to really hear, see, or feel anything. We talk over people, watch TV while we eat, and worry while we're going to sleep. As with any way of being that we become accustomed to, all this speed trickles down to young people as the norm of society. As we breed intolerance for silence and stillness in our lives, we bleed out sophistication and self-reflection. We don't want to delve into the subtleties of life; we want to be distracted. As Kurt Cobain said, "We feel stupid and contagious—Here we are now, entertain us!"

Appreciating and practicing stillness can bring our activity into balance. Stillness is not just flopping. In a sense, it's a very active practice because it disrupts our habitual busy-ness. It's about learning to let go of our mental agenda so that we can be open, receptive, quiet, and clear. When we are still, our senses open and the world introduces itself to us, just as when we sit still and quiet in the forest and eventually the forest animals come along. If we sit in the same place for a few days we begin to see more: how the moss changes, where the fox runs, how the little trees grow in the sun patches. Being still brings a sense of being centered. Rather than chasing each little task and thought, we discover the experience of being in one place. Wherever we are is our place in that moment. We find that we belong there. That singularity aligns us with our natural, open awareness of the world around us. Therefore, stillness is aliveness.

Meditation is the essential practice of stillness. In meditation we sit in a chair or cross-legged on a cushion or on the earth. For a period of time—maybe five minutes, or longer once we get used to it—we sit still. We make a decision to be in one place, and though it may not seem like much, this is a very powerful decision. It goes against the whole rushing current of speed and momentum within and around us. In that moment we become our own teacher, the kindest teacher, who gives us what we need. We are offering ourselves stillness, quiet, and space to simply be with ourselves as we are. We are teaching ourselves to trust in just being human.

If we sit in a relaxed but awake manner we soon find that stillness is not static but full of feelings and energy. We are not garden statues of Buddha. We have sensations, thoughts, and movement. We breathe and our bodies expand and relax. We blink and shift our posture to find balance and ease. As beginners we tend to feel quite antsy and fidgety, like children in the midst of a too-long lecture. But with practice we settle down. Being still begins to feel natural rather than feeling like an exotic exercise.

One traditional word for describing meditation is *familiarity*. By holding our attention to something, we become familiar with it. Essentially, we are becoming familiar with ourselves. By sitting with ourselves we are allowing the rushing waters of our attention to slow and sink into the earth, nourishing the ecosystem of our body and mind. We are becoming familiar with the elemental qualities of our humanity. In a sense, we are becoming reacquainted with ourselves after a long separation. We have been away, across an ocean of distraction, but we are coming home.

As we become familiar with stillness, at first it feels quite separate from our life of work, teaching, to-do lists, and so on. Even when meditators go on retreat and find a peaceful respite from the speed and claustrophobia of things, they are often disappointed by how quickly they get swept right back into it upon returning to active life. This is normal, and it's why we need to incorporate stillness into our lives in an ongoing and natural way. Meditation practice should be like drinking water. We don't just drink a whole lake during the summer and ignore it the rest of the time—we need to drink a little bit everyday.[9] In that way we gradually become more familiar with stillness. We are becoming acquainted with the natural stillness that is waiting within us like the depth of the ocean beneath the waves. Our body is beginning to synchronize with that underlying peacefulness.

Then we can begin to enter into the world of activity, maybe even the classroom, with a sense of ceremony. Like bugaku dancers we can begin to utilize stillness to bring out the beauty and confidence in each action.

Detention:

Sit still.

As a first step toward developing a meditation practice, experiment with stillness. If we have been brought up to "stay busy" or are used to filling our time with noise and activity, this may be a challenge.

We are putting our speedy, anxious parts in detention, asking them to temporarily chill out and make space for other parts of our being. Sometimes this feels like suddenly getting off a moving train—we can still sense the momentum of our activities, our urge to be productive, and our active thought process rushing through us. This is not a problem. Just sit still with whatever is happening.

❖ **Sit for a few minutes in your meditation spot.** Put your phone in a different room and make sure you don't have any distractions at hand. Sit with a straight back and relaxed shoulders, eyes open, and do nothing. Don't even try to calm your mind or meditate. Just see how it feels to be still. Don't be rigid; just let your body rest. Breathe naturally. What do you notice?

❖ **Find opportunities to rest in stillness during your day.** It could be a few seconds at a red light, or while waiting in line at the bank. Rather than turning on the radio or checking your email, do nothing. What do you notice?

❖ **Find opportunities to be still in the midst of the school day.** Maybe this is while children are playing and you are watching from the sideline, or while they are working and you have a minute when no one needs your attention, or when you are off duty. Allow your body to be quiet. Briefly turn off your teacher goggles—that part of your training that scans for trouble or students that need your attention—and just observe in a neutral, open way. What do you notice?

{ Mindfulness }

"The faculty of voluntarily bringing back a wandering attention, over and over again, is the very root of judgment, character and will. An education which will improve this faculty would be *the* education *par excellence*."[10] —William James

Attention has always been a key factor in learning, but prior to the emergence of the mindfulness movement in schools, practical instruction in *how* to work with our attention has rarely been offered. Today, mindfulness techniques are widely introduced as a way of strengthening attention, reducing anxiety, and developing self-awareness, all of which can benefit teachers and students on many levels. In the Shambhala tradition, mindfulness is utilized as a way of revealing basic goodness. For teachers, mindfulness practice can be a means of cultivating our whole being—body, heart, and mind. In the classroom and in life, it is an anchor, a sane and stable reference point to return to, whatever weather may come.

Mindfulness is not really a technique or a trick; it's a natural aspect of our minds. Basically, it is the mind's ability to know where it is. So if we're tasting a blueberry, we are actually tasting it. We're not absorbed in fantasies about making blueberry pie or memories of picking blueberries as a child. We are there, tasting that very blueberry. When our mind is not trained, our mindfulness is weak, and therefore we are easily lost in distraction and much of our true experience is lost. Through meditation we can develop our mind's ability to settle and to remain. This makes the mind stable, clear, and strong.

When our attention is scattered our mind feels fragmented. We become lost in our head and disconnected from our bodies, our environment, and the wisdom of basic goodness. On the other hand, when we gather our attention and allow our mind to rest, it naturally settles in the present and comes into a sense of fullness. Fostering mindfulness is healing for the mind. Stress and anxiety arise from fixating on the past and worrying about the future. Through developing the ability to bring our mind into the present, we gain insight into those states of distraction. We see that being endlessly caught up in our thoughts is harmful to us, and furthermore, unnecessary. We begin to see that we are not made up of our thought-clusters, and we don't necessarily have to believe or play out the narratives and stories we weave in our heads. We feel a sense of relief and simplicity. We can just be here.

Mindfulness is being present and aware with whatever is arising. This does not mean that our minds have to be blank or in some kind of ethereal "Zen" state. Mindfulness includes being present with our thoughts and emotions. If we are feeling speedy and worried and hungry, we can feel those things presently. We don't have to ward them off. Rather, we experience them without added on layers of mental commentary, panic, complaint, or distraction.

With mindfulness we observe our thoughts and experiences without judgment. If we feel angry, we allow ourselves to experience the textures and qualities of that emotion. We stay with the feelings in our bodies. We do not get wrapped up in the story of what provoked our anger, nor do we tell ourselves that being angry is bad and try to push the feeling away. Applying mindfulness could be as simple as recognizing our feeling and saying to ourselves, "This is anger."

This sense of spacious observation should not be thought of as detachment, however. Mindfulness is not a tool that we use to separate from ourselves, but a means of developing warmth. We can practice being mindful of our experiences like a loving mother caring for her child. She is naturally present and attentive with her child in all that it does. She protects it from harm and directs it toward growth.[11] In this way, we are not emotionless in our practice of developing a stable and healthy mind; we are human, caring, and good.

In meditation we nurture mindfulness by gently bringing our attention into the present moment. Our foundation for this is the stillness of our posture. Sitting and settling allows us to feel how we are. As we feel what is arising in our experience—warmth, coolness, tingling, heaviness, light, sound, and so on—we naturally arrive *here*, and our scattered attention is gathered back into the present.

Traditionally, we use the breath as a further reference point to anchor our attention. We feel the breath as it moves in our bodies. When we notice that our mind has wandered, as it inevitably does, we simply bring our attention back to the breath. As we feel this very breath, we return to our sense of feeling and being in the present. Eventually we zone out again—a fantasy or a memory hooks our minds for either a short or long while—and then at some point we notice that we're lost in thought. Once again, we gently but deliberately bring our attention back to the breath. Again and again, we practice in this way for as long as our session lasts. In this simple way we become familiar with ourselves, foster trust, practice friendliness, and train in mindfulness.

All manner of thoughts arise when we sit in meditation. We have outlandish thoughts, dull thoughts, inspirational thoughts, silly thoughts, violent thoughts, sexual thoughts, and so forth. As these thoughts come and go, sometimes they expand into emotions. As we sit we may suddenly find ourselves immersed in anger, sinking in boredom, caught in anxiety, or captivated by passion. A key instruction is to sit like a mountain with all of these thoughts and emotions. Waves of feelings swell up and subside, but whatever arises we don't get carried away. Even if we have a splendiferous inspiration, we don't get up to write it down. We are learning to abide, to remain. We don't evaluate our thoughts as good thoughts or bad thoughts. We are developing equanimity toward our thoughts, and in a sense, dismantling their ability to hook us into habitual reactions.

Through training in this way we don't necessarily have fewer thoughts and emotions, but gradually we learn to remain present when they arise. Our attention becomes less like a feather blown by the wind of habit. Our thoughts hold less sway over us. Because we begin to understand them as ephemeral and passing, they begin to lose their ability to draw us into neurotic tangles.

By fully meeting our thoughts and emotions in meditation we are training to meet the world with open eyes and hearts. Our life is full of energy, just like our mind. We could see our students as personifications of our own thoughts and feelings—Dylan is just like our timidity, Chandali is our anger, Sara is our anxiety, Timothy is our weird randomness, and so on. Rather than being thrown from our horse by the energy of others, we can stay in the saddle of the present moment as we relate with each student, colleague, or parent. We've learned to be gentle and attentive to the energy of our own minds. Now we can be with the energy of others, remaining open, grounded, and inquisitive.

Does this sound like an impossible ideal? None of us can transform ourselves overnight. We've been swimming in the current of personal and cultural habit patterns for a long time. Truthfully, just *noticing* when we've been caught up in fixation is the awakening of mindfulness. Transforming the mind and heart is a lifelong journey, but it's made up of many beginnings. Whatever happens, don't be discouraged. That's another key instruction from the masters of the past. Just start fresh.

Study Notes:

Meditation posture:

- ❖ Natural, straight back—as though your head is holding up the sky
- ❖ Relaxed shoulders
- ❖ Legs loosely crossed if you're sitting on a meditation cushion, or with feet on the floor if you're in a chair
- ❖ Hands resting on thighs, palms down
- ❖ Eyes open, soft gaze, looking down about 4 or 5 feet in front

- ❖ Feel a grounded connection to the earth below, and a spacious sense of the sky above
- ❖ Feel a sense of dignity and ease in your body as you sit like a mountain

Note: A little discomfort is natural, but if something hurts, adjust your posture or rest. Don't make it an endurance test. Be kind to your body.

Meditation Attitude:

- ❖ Gentleness
- ❖ Trust
- ❖ Care
- ❖ Vulnerability

Meditation Technique:

- ❖ Breathe naturally
- ❖ Feel the breath as it moves in your body
- ❖ Place your attention gently on the breath
- ❖ When your attention is carried away into fantasy or distraction, notice that, and then simply bring your attention back to the feeling of the breath

Balance in Equal Parts:

- ❖ Body: Feeling
- ❖ Attitude: Warmth
- ❖ Attention: Fresh start each time
- ❖ Curiosity: Openness to whatever arises

Homework:

Begin a regular meditation practice. Sit for a manageable period of time each day, and start with four or five days each week. Ten minutes is good to start. If that's feeling good, you can increase to fifteen, then twenty or thirty. It's helpful to sit at the same time each day.[12]

Presence

Okay, Pop Quiz!

1. Which word best describes a good teacher?
    A. Skillful
    B. Charismatic
    C. Genuine
    D. Cantankerous

Don't be too quick to rule out D! There are some teachers who really make grumpiness work for them. But probably if you were in the classroom you would raise your hand and ask if you can circle more than one answer, right? What if you could only pick one? Let's break it down.

Skill is clearly essential. Teaching is a craft as well as an art. One can learn and master the praxes that define good instruction, classroom management, lesson planning, and so on. This is important, because many people think teaching is a kind of magic. Great teachers have a sort of mythos around them—their skill seems to be an ineffable product of their character.[13] But effective teaching can be developed through method and experience.

Charisma can't hurt. Some of my most memorable teachers had interesting and entertaining personalities, like Mr. Johnson who would do things like stash a tape player with a recording of a dog barking in the ceiling vent. About ten minutes into class the barking would start echoing through the vent and Mr. J would whack the ceiling with his yardstick and mutter, "It's the dogs again…" It was weird and hilarious and made me love him. But the desire to be a charismatic teacher can be a red herring. School has become so famously boring that there's a high premium put on engaging students. Engagement is critical, but teachers shouldn't act like entertainers. We all want to be the fun teacher, but there's nothing worse than the teacher who tries too hard to be liked. Admittedly, I was a few years into my teaching career before I stopped imitating Mr. J. At some point the act ran out of juice.

Probably the best answer, if we can only pick one, is "C." Genuineness. Rather than relying on our teacher skills alone, or on any kind of fabricated personality, we can learn to be ourselves. It may sound sappy, but naturalness is an increasingly rare quality. We are living in a time when being obsessed with our own constructed appearance is the norm. We have new ways to design our personalities through what we post, like, and share online, and the boundary between online and "real" life is often blurry. When we're insecure we become more fixated on our clothing, jokes, cronies, credentials, and plans to shore us up. Our desire to be liked outsizes our ability to be ourselves.

When we trust ourselves, we don't need to convince anyone of our validity. We might fear that if we don't put on a show we will become bland and invisible. Instead, we find that relaxation with ourselves taps us into a wellspring of energy and care. Being genuine sustains us. We may be busy, but our attention isn't scattered.

Therefore, we become more available to others. We develop a natural sense of presence that is warm and strong.

A genuine presence is not something we put on like armor. It's not a skill that we can learn to perform as part of our teaching repertoire. It's important to be good at our jobs, but if we try to hide within our role, we just find ourselves perpetuating a façade. Then we end up working all the time at keeping up the image of what kind of teacher we are, and we go home exhausted. A strong, clear, and healthy presence is not something we fabricate, but a natural radiance that comes from a person whose body and mind are at ease.

This naturalness is essential when it comes to creating culture in our classroom. The quality of our presence is at least as important as the lessons we give or how we teach them. Human beings naturally mirror each other and absorb the feeling of each other's way of being, which is communicated through body language, bearing, tone of voice, and in many other subtle ways. Being genuine and present with our students communicates with the genuineness in them. We are transmitting the *feeling* of being human, and as Maya Angelou said, "People will forget what you said, people will forget what you did, but people will never forget how you made them feel."[14] That's where the real teaching takes place.

When our mind is scattered and our body is agitated we do have a presence of sorts—or maybe we could call it an absence—that affects how others feel. A few years ago I had lunch with an old friend who had become quite successful in his career. He was working hard and it was paying off, but during our lunch he was completely distracted. His phone constantly interrupted us with texts and calls, which he always responded to, at least by looking at the phone, and he was always networking—chatting up the restaurant staff and whoever else was around. I was happy that his work was flourishing, but at the end of our lunch I felt discouraged. We had met for lunch, but only part of him had shown up for me. I also felt sad to know that this had become the new normal for him. It was almost like my old friend was gone, and I wasn't sure whether or not I would see him again.

Our presence is an expression of our inner life. When we meet someone's eyes, we get a feeling for their state of mind. How a person holds herself, grooms, dresses, moves, speaks, and rests also communicates this ineffable but palpable quality. When we meet someone who has developed herself in a genuine way, her presence is stable, accommodating, gentle, and radiant, like a mountain. When we gaze upon a mountain we feel a natural sense of respect, as well as inspiration. Have you had a person in your life who you felt that way about?

One such person for me was Kanjuro Shibata, Sensei XX. For many years, starting when I was about 12 years old, I practiced Kyūdo, the Way of the Bow, or what is often called Zen Archery, a form of meditation with traditional Japanese bow and arrows. Shibata Sensei was a twentieth generation Kyūdo master and bow-maker to the Emperor of Japan who moved to Boulder, Colorado to teach Shambhala students. I remember watching him incessantly when I was young. He would preside over Kyūdo class, watching the students from his chair, peering out from under his bushy eyebrows with his hands resting on his walking stick that was made from a broken bow. He didn't always do very much, but I was always absorbing his presence, fascinated at first by his samurai demeanor, but more deeply transfixed by his inner power.

Embodiment

A genuine teacher is very real and very deep, but the power of their presence isn't actually that mysterious. Genuine presence has two aspects: embodiment and motivation. Embodiment is like the solidity of the mountain. When a person's meditation has sunk in and become natural, they embody it. Teaching is often thought of as a mental activity, but it becomes human and real when the teacher embodies genuineness.

An embodied presence arises when the mind comes home to the body. Then we feel grounded, and our attention rests in the present. Awareness saturates the body, and the mind settles. We could call this natural mindfulness, or maybe natural bodyfulness. Either way, there is a feeling of fullness. Our feet are on the floor, our mind is open, we are *there*, and therefore we can be present with our students. There is a sense of potency, a feeling of priority in the moment, as well as ease. Our body and mind are harmonized, which gives us a natural presence.

School Bell:

❖ Think of your body as a beautiful offering of presence to your students.

❖ Work with your posture. Sit or stand with relaxed dignity. Come back to your posture throughout the day.

❖ Use the feeling of being in your body as an anchor to the present moment.

❖ When the school bell rings, rediscover your body. Let your attention drop in to your whole body. Feel your bodily sensations: Feet on the floor, bum on the chair, pencil in hand, etc. Allow your senses to open. Feel your breath. Use other reminders throughout the day to come back to embodiment.[15]

{ Motivation }

Here's another story. Jamie was a high school student I taught a while back. Jamie was shy and skittish and didn't really know how to be around people her own age. She felt more comfortable with adults, and so would seek out the company of the teachers during most of the breaks. Jamie was sweet, but a bit lonely and cloying. Sometimes when I saw her coming I would swivel in my desk chair to face my computer, or get busy marking some papers so that I would have an excuse not to make room for her. I suppose my own mindfulness came into play, to the small extent that I noticed what I was doing. I began to reflect on how I was reacting to Jamie, and I discovered that I wasn't considering her at all. I was only thinking about what I felt like doing. This leads to the second value in the presence equation: motivation.

In any activity we engage in we could ask ourselves what our motivation is. Where are we coming from? We could ask, "Why am I doing this?" We might have to ask the question again, and then again, in order to get down to the root, the real motivation. If we're eating a pear we might peer into our motivation. On the surface we think we're hungry, but looking more deeply we find that we aren't really hungry, we just wanted something sweet and juicy because we were getting anxious while paying the bills. Our motivation is to soothe ourselves.

The purpose of this introspection is not to develop cynicism toward ourselves, or to constantly interrogate our motives. It's to become familiar with ourselves in a deeper way. There's nothing wrong with longing for the comfort of a juicy pear. As we inquire into our motivation around various parts of our life we can be gentle and appreciative of whatever we notice. We will find that where we're coming from is layered and amorphous. It shifts from day to day and throughout each day. We may discover a sense of duty or a sense of inspiration drawing us forward, or that we are mostly coming from laziness, or that fear, love, or ambition is the most compelling factor at the heart of our motivation.

Take a moment to ask yourself:
Why did you become a teacher?
Why are you a teacher now?

Some of the teachers I've spoken with say their answers to these two questions are the same, but most notice that they haven't thought about it much since before they began their career. Reflecting now, they notice that their motivation is not static. They may have lost track of their original motivation, or they may find that it has evolved and matured. Some feel teaching is a sacred calling—that this path chose them, rather than the other way around. Even if this is so, discovering meaningful motivation is a day-to-day practice. Just as our habitual patterns work to cover over our inherently bright and open hearts, our habits of self-fixation—as well as frustrations and cynicism in our jobs, the ingratitude or apathy of our students, and the judgment of our critics—can back us into a corner. Our sense of motivation shrinks into a little ball. We find we're just trying to get by, cruising under the radar until we get to go home. But we can work with our motivation. Each day we can reflect on it and breathe life into it. We can free ourselves from the burden of fear and boredom, and open up to the motivation of our heart, which is boundless and full of tenderness.

Teaching is a rich field of practice, and we may find many deep wells of motivation when we contemplate why we teach. We might reflect on the joys of teaching, the pleasure of spending time with young people, the satisfaction of seeing them learn and smile and mature. We might reflect on our teaching subjects and their potential to help our students be prepared for life. We may also notice that we are motivated by a desire to impress our students, our colleagues, and our friends by being great teachers. We may notice our desire for our students to connect with us and look up to us. We may find ourselves feeling like the reasons why we teach no longer hold the life-giving water of meaning and inspiration they once did. When we begin our practice of working with motivation, we start by simply looking into how we feel and noticing with curiosity what arises. We don't need to evaluate or judge what we find. We're simply checking in with ourselves, like a runner considering his energy level before going on a run.

Having gained a sense of where our motivation is on that day, we can begin to expand it. We all have a tendency to collapse inward, to shrink into self-preoccupation. So we begin with a small motivation—our thoughts and actions are primarily arising from self-concern. We are interested in amusing, nurturing, and protecting ourselves. This small motivation can be grotesque if we become so engrossed in our own self-interest that we can't see the people and world around us. But it can also be perfectly healthy. We need to care for ourselves, rest, exercise, learn, and play. There's nothing wrong if we notice that our thoughts are in orbit around our own needs. It may mean we are being called to respond to ourselves, to offer ourselves space, practice, gentleness, reflection, or inspiration. This first level of motivation is not bad, but it is small because it's turned inward.

A greater level of motivation arises when we begin to consider others. As teachers, this primarily means our students, but certainly includes their parents, our colleagues, the greater community, and ultimately everyone, the eco-system, the planet. It begins with the simple step of including another person, in this case let's say one student, and considering what would be good for her. Just that thought process creates an important shift. We've begun to expand our circle, to open our attention outward.

Part of what brings beauty and meaning to teaching is that it naturally involves turning our attention to others, evoking a sense of care and service. However, we should watch out for a tricky twist: Sometimes we only consider our students through a professional lens. We think of them only as student-units, not as human beings. We see them as our project. Thus, we may be thinking of how to help them, but our motivation has more to do with ourselves and our desire for success in our work. We become wrapped up in their successes and failures not because we care so much about them, but because we want them to reflect well on us. If we notice this tendency in our motivation, we can reflect on our student again, remembering that he is a human being who experiences a full range of suffering and joy. Then we can open our mind to his genuine benefit.

We might contemplate one student, and then another, or we might contemplate a whole class. As we do so, we consider their happiness, their growth, their flourishing. We can recall their intrinsic goodness, that brilliance and softness within them. We are shifting the focus of our small motivation, expanding it to include others. We may have no idea *how* to help our students, or give them happiness, but that doesn't matter right now. The purpose of this contemplation is to open our true teacher's heart, which longs to serve, and which takes delight in others.

When we have this greater level of motivation, it helps us. If we wake up tired, our own concerns can weigh us down, making us feel heavy and depressed. But when our heart is in service to others, we get up. When our motivation is to attend to others, we look out and see them. Our sphere of awareness is bigger.

When I noticed that I was intentionally shutting out Jamie, I had to rouse a greater motivation, expanding beyond my own cocoon. I began to turn toward her, and to just be with her when she came to visit. I let go of my own agenda, which made me feel more relaxed, and I began to appreciate Jamie's company. Some of the other teachers worked with her in a similar way, and she in turn began to relax and mature, even dropping some of her nervous habits.

Practicing presence with our students is like holding a cup of tea. In Japanese tea ceremony, you receive tea in a handcrafted ceramic bowl. Kneeling on the mat, you pick up the bowl and hold it with two hands. Turning it on your palm you appreciate the tea bowl, including its beautiful imperfections. Offering presence to our students is holding them with two hands. With mindfulness we bring ourselves into the moment so that our attention doesn't spill. With a sense of genuine motivation we attend to our students from the heart, appreciating their inherent worthiness. Knowing goodness in ourselves we feel relaxed and full. Trusting the goodness in our students, we are happy to serve.

If we teach, let us teach this way.

Self-Assessment:

Take a few minutes to contemplate and expand your motivation. This exercise can be good to do anytime, but may be especially potent first thing in the morning, or just before you go to sleep:

- ❖ In your teaching life right now, what do you care about? Reflect gently. Allow yourself to delve a bit deeper than the short-term things—catching up on marking, scheduling a parent meeting, planning tomorrow's classes, etc. Underneath those things, where are you really coming from?
- ❖ Generate a feeling of caring and positive motivation toward yourself. Spend a minute or so simply wishing positive things for yourself—that you will have energy and be free of fear; that you will flourish in your work, etc. Notice how contemplating in this way makes you feel.
- ❖ Expand your motivation by turning your thoughts to others. Think of a student who you feel concerned about. Generate the wish for them to succeed, to be safe, and to be happy.
- ❖ Extend the feeling of benevolence to your whole class. Open your true teacher's heart and let it melt any cynicism and frustration that arise when you think of your students.

Reflect on their basic goodness and feel longing for their goodness to blossom. Wish for them to be free of anxiety and fear, and to discover the joys of learning.

❖ After contemplating in this way, let go of the thought process and rest for a few seconds, just noticing how you feel.

PART III: TEACHING LIKE A RIVER

Friendship and care are essential to us as human beings. Without them we become isolated, dry, and brittle. These vital elements flow through our teaching when we let them. Genuine teaching is a river that nourishes us—both teachers and students—with the waters of life and connection.

Empathy

Education doesn't end when school is out. It's a continual process for all of us, an uncontrolled experiment in the classroom of our lives. We learn as we live. But what we learn, and how we learn, may or may not be helpful or true. My friend Michelle King, who teaches middle school in Pittsburgh, gave a talk in which she asked a simple but key question: "Does education do for us what we need it to do?" What do we, the people of the world, living in this time, need education to do? Is it helping us learn in ways that open our hearts and minds, or are we learning in ways that calcify us with fear and prejudice?

Our purpose as teachers is to educate and to facilitate learning; if we don't help our students learn, we fall short. But when we narrow our scope down to that fine point alone, we can lose a sense of perspective. Even if we successfully facilitate learning, are we fostering an education that nurtures the world, or are we perpetuating a world of selfishness and materialism?

Education is not only about accumulating knowledge and skills. Learning is a natural and ongoing part of life. As children grow they are constantly interacting with their universe—developing a feeling and an understanding, for better or worse, about who they are and about their world.[16] What we teach our students is only a tiny fraction of the education they absorb through all of their senses and experiences, and what we can measure of their learning is even smaller. While our jobs may only hold us accountable for the measurable bit, if we think the rest doesn't matter we default to a very narrow purpose in our work. Viewing our students' success only within the tiny spectrum of their grades leads us to become functionaries, moving our students along the conveyor belt. Our purpose becomes to "pass" them to the next station in life, until they are trained enough to be functionaries themselves. This mentality doesn't suit the love of learning and awakening that most of us cherish. Still, all too often, teachers are confined to being mere stewards of the *status quo*.

For many teachers, these limitations are embodied in the school system. "I love my students," teachers often say, "but I hate the system." There is clearly a need for reform in the school system, and its shortcomings are responsible for much of the daily overwhelm and burnout of teachers. But we also need to recognize that the *status quo* is a reflection of our collective social outlook. We could even say it is what we have been educated to produce. If we wish to see genuine transformation, we need new learning, which means we'll need to look inward as well as outward. We can't just blame the system. We need a new vision, and we need to practice living that vision from the inside out while we work to understand and change the broken culture and structures that surround us.

The central lesson, the deeply embedded value, of *status quo* education is individualism. It is the paradigm of separation, an invisible system that puts self-interest above all other interests. Within this paradigm we feel the need to promote and protect ourselves and we constantly compare ourselves with others. This outlook leads to a feeling of isolation and a culture of materialism (building ourselves up), aggression (cutting others down), and apathy. When we learn within a framework of individualism we become increasingly fearful, hardened against the world, and willing to ignore its cries for help. Even though it's about maintaining business-as-usual, the *status quo* doesn't progress in a straight line; it's an inward-tightening spiral.

The antidote to individualism, the spiral that opens our hearts and minds outwards, is empathy. "We are naturally empathic beings," says Michelle King, "but do our institutions remind us to be that way? Do our interactions remind us to be that way? Does education remind us to be that way?" Empathy is what we feel when we relax our fixation on self. It's the experience of letting ourselves mingle with others. Like a drop of watercolor on wet paper, with empathy we soften, expand, and blur into our world. Empathy is what allows us to be touched, to feel, to taste, to appreciate. It's being moved by a piece of beautiful poetry, or snagged by the hook of a good rhythm. It's being unstuck, unbounded by the project of maintaining "me." It's feeling the flow of communication, the living river of life that we all are in together.

Many of us have a strong sense of empathy and care for our students, which is why we teach. It's what impels us to find ways to help our students, often beyond the bounds of duty. In some ways, this is the true beauty of teaching. At the same time, like other caregivers, many teachers struggle with the impact of feeling such care ongoing. It's difficult to absorb the reality of our students' lives when they face painful situations. Knowing that they may lack any meaningful support at home can be lonely knowledge to bear.

Especially for teachers whose students are dealing with trauma or the effects of social ills like racism or poverty, caring can lead to exhaustion, self-sacrifice, guilt, depression, anger, and numbness.[17]

Faced with this challenge, it may seem that the options are either to care less or to keep caring more, even if it tears us apart. Welcome to school...would you like spiritual death or martyrdom? Perhaps we could find an approach with a bit more balance. Balance is not so much about having less or more of any particular feeling, but in having the capacity to hold and care for our own experience, whatever it may be, moment to moment. We need a container that is large enough and strong enough to hold the feelings that come at us and arise within us.

Working with our experience in the stillness of meditation creates a basis of self-awareness and care, grounded in the physical body. This anchors us to the present. Gentleness, warmth, and mindfulness lead to a key insight—that our thoughts don't have to dominate our experience. We find that thoughts and feelings arise naturally, but we can also allow them to go naturally. As we become more familiar with this grounded awareness, and with the coming and going of our mind's contents, we become less like a vacuum bag that fills up with thoughts. We feel less afraid of our thoughts and feelings. We realize that we always have the ability to return to the simplicity of this moment and to the sensations in our body. This helps us open to ourselves, and then to others, without losing our sense of wellbeing and perspective.[18]

This is helpful, because caring is actually choiceless. As Michelle said, we are empathic beings. We are, in our basic humanity, open and connected to what we experience. Not feeling—shutting down and numbing ourselves to life—is an unnatural tendency. It is a function of individualism, a means of projecting boundaries in the absence of trust. We do this all the time as a matter of habit, but before we go numb, we always feel. Before we judge the world, we feel it. That feeling is basic goodness. It comes before the conceptual marmalade we spread on our experience, but it isn't a dull state like plain toast—it has a natural sense of warmth and care, a sense of aliveness. That's empathy.

Connecting with this undercurrent of warmth in relationship with others does not mean that we understand what our students are feeling, or why they feel what they do. Imagining that we know the experience of others can be quite problematic, especially if our students come from a different social context than ours. If we project our ideas—even our good-hearted ones—onto others, we may just be boxing them up with our preconceptions. In this case, it's more that we feel our own human aliveness—our pain and sadness, as well as our joy and delight—and we feel the aliveness of others. We may not know *what* they feel, but we feel *that* they feel. That makes us soft and curious.

Empathy connects us to society. Society—ourselves and our world *together*—is the reality of our existence. As much as we try to fortify ourselves as individuals, we never actually achieve isolation. We are interwoven with our world. We are immersed in society. From the sound of traffic outside the window to our glimpse of the stars twinkling in the sky, we *are* society, and empathy is the river of feeling that flows through us. Willingness to touch that experience breaks through our barriers and alienation. It dissolves what separates us from each other, and from our world.

Education and empathy come together when we embrace the experience of teaching as communion, being in society, with our students. I see this simple, often invisible act as a powerful gesture of revolution. We are reversing the spiral of the *status quo*. We are standing up for the heart in defiance of all that tries to close it, and for society in defiance of all that tells us it's not worthy of our care.

Cooking Class:

Empathy Soup:
During study or naptime, a passing period, recess, lunch, or another time when the focus of the class is not on you, contemplate natural empathy.

- ❖ **Begin by connecting to yourself.** Notice how you feel in your body and emotional state. Tune into your sense perceptions, allowing your senses to receive the environment.
- ❖ **Open your awareness to your class.** Feel the living energy of the class—all of the students, their personal expressions, their bodies, their personalities, their stories, their struggles, their breath, their feelings—like a cauldron bubbling with humanity. Attune yourself to the feeling of this little human society.
- ❖ **Jump into the cauldron.** Let go of a feeling of being separate from the energy of the group. Melt into the soup. Allow a feeling of warmth and care to flow.

Class Dismissed:

It can be good to think about—and even worry about—our students. We feel their humanity, hear their stories, and feel care and empathy. However, sometimes we get filled up with stories and our system becomes overwhelmed. It's important to learn how to let go of thoughts about our students in order to reconnect with our own basic health. Try this:

❖ At the end of the day, spend five or ten minutes in meditation.

❖ As the thoughts and feelings of the day swirl around in your mind, gently bring your attention into your body.

❖ If placing attention on the breath feels too raw and tender, let your attention gently touch other parts of the body—maybe feeling your feet on the floor, your palms on your thighs, or your legs on your seat.

❖ Give yourself permission to release your students from your mind, knowing that you still care for them and will return to them later.

❖ Don't try to push out thoughts and worries. Simply ground yourself by feathering your attention lightly into your physical sensations. Allow the body to soothe the mind.

{ Friendship }

When we talk about education, we are not talking purely in terms of making the illiterate literate. We're not particularly talking about a learning process which constantly delivers a tremendous slap on the face and exposes your stupidity, a process in which the more you're confronted with learned people, the more stupid you feel. We're not talking about education as a form of insult to the learner. That has been the problem all along. The form of education we're talking about is a celebration... The teacher's attitude is no longer that he or she is dealing with ignorant people, but instead that he is dealing with tremendous intelligence on the student's part. Some kind of spark is taking place, some new form of friendship. So the teacher and the student form a tremendous friendship.—Chögyam Trungpa, *Education for An Enlightened Society*[19]

One day a couple of years ago, my seven-year-old son Gabriel was having a rough morning. He was very upset and was making a lot of trouble for me as I struggled to wrangle him and his sister through our morning routine and get them to school. He cried all the way to his classroom where his teacher, Mrs. Williams, met us at the door. I was cooked by then and ready to hand him off so that I could get to my own classroom to get ready for teaching. Mrs. Williams looked at the two of us, then took Gabe into her arms and said, "It's ok Gabe. I'm sad today too." That melted him—he softened and relaxed. It melted me too. I was amazed to see that such a simple gesture was needed in that moment, and that I, in my preoccupation, was unable to offer it to my son. But I also felt the simple goodness and warmth that Mrs. Williams invoked in the moment. She was willing to be human with Gabe and to express that as kindness. Certainly she was being a good teacher, but it was her empathy and friendship that restored wellbeing to the situation. Friendship is an essential principle in genuine education. It's how we move from a dry, transactional approach to an empathic, societal one.

For some teachers the notion of friendship brings up questions. Is it really our job to be friends with our students? Don't their peers fulfill that need? Isn't it our role to teach and provide discipline? It's nice when our students like us, but we all know there will be students who can't stand us—are we supposed to worry about that? Is it even appropriate to be friends with our students? These are all valid questions and point to the need for a deeper understanding of what we mean by friendship here.

Generally, we can't really be pals with our students in the way we are friends with our peers. It tends to confuse the natural hierarchy of the teacher–student relationship. But there is another way of experiencing friendship. In the Shambhala tradition it is said that just as humanity is basically good, society is also basically good. Even though society is rife with problems, at its heart there is health, openness, and wisdom. As human beings, our primary connection with others is not rejection or distrust. When we experience another person, our first flash is openness and natural curiosity. In that primary space of relationship, we feel warmth and possibility. Even when people hate each other, at the heart of the relationship, underneath the fear, blame, and judgment, there is a yearning to communicate. That fundamental care and openness is basic goodness. Friendship is what happens when we connect with that goodness in our experience of being with others. It's the natural and simple feeling of being with another person, feeling our existence together and our longing to share understanding. I think of it as "returning to friendship," because it has to do with appreciating the humanity of others, which was always there. It's like discovering a river flowing beneath the earth.

There is always a connection between human beings. We may teach in a huge classroom and not even know our students' names, but simply by perceiving the fact of each other's existence, we are connected. We form society. Returning to friendship is a practice of honoring and protecting that relationship.

Society and communities today suffer from complex problems— from systemic injustice to classroom conflict. To address these issues, we need some kind of square one. If we don't even want to feel the energy of being in simple existence with one another, it will be very difficult to unravel our more complicated challenges. It is said that basic goodness is the ground of all virtues. Therefore, simply appreciating another human being allows kindness, generosity, patience, joy, and humility to arise. Friendship and empathy nurture and heal us. On the other hand, isolation and separation degrade society. Fostering distrust, we become more afraid, angry, and feeble as a society. Rejection and conflict arise. The walls of separation grow thicker. In each moment of relationship with another person we have a choice: either default to separation, or practice friendship.

Practicing friendship means deciding to be in society with others. We decide to feel ourselves in relationship to our students, respecting our shared humanity in the moment. It is a practice of being open, being *with* rather than apart. We don't fortify ourselves within the walls of our role, or limit our awareness to the transaction of business between us. Of course, we still have to fulfill our role. We have to be a teacher to our students. But we don't act out our role as a mere performance. Even good actors don't simply perform— they act as though the audience isn't there, and yet they stay utterly connected with their audience. Audience and actor may even begin to breathe in unison.

If this all sounds a bit easy to say, I can assure you, a great many of the interactions I have with my teenage students are terse, frustrating, and awkward. As often as my classes are connected, fun, and inspiring, they can feel distracted and wild, or semi-comatose, depressed, and flat. Sometimes I feel as though I'm hosting a party, but only prisoners showed up. Individual interactions can be lifeless and perfunctory. For example, I ask Scott to check in about the class he missed and I begin to explain things to him, but when I look into his face I get the distinct feeling he's just waiting for me to stop talking so he can get on with the parts of his life he cares about. Slightly deflated, I pare down my agenda, reducing the conversation to a minimal function of making sure he knows what to do with an assignment. I ask if he understands, which he does, so I end by saying "ok," and he walks away without saying anything. This sort of interaction tends to discourage me from seeking a dynamic, living connection with Scott or my other students. The next time I speak with Scott I might be that much more transactional, with less eye contact, humor, empathy, or openness.

On the other hand, if I commit to practicing friendship rather than beginning from a place of separateness, I can tune into the living energy that is already flowing between us. I commit to being with Scott. I look at him and open myself to him, not analyzing, but perceiving and feeling. I'm becoming available to the communication that is always present, flowing like a river. It's like the feeling we experience holding hands, or standing in the sunshine, feeling the warmth and taking in the pure, bright light. This communication isn't playing on the words channel; it's music playing on the basic goodness channel. We listen to it with our senses and from the open space of our being. Whether or not I even like Scott is secondary. I don't have to like him to be in friendship with him. Our conversation may play out in the same way. On the other hand, because I am actually listening, more possibilities become available. I might notice a hint of overwhelm in his bearing. I ask him if he's worried about anything and a little shift takes place. He says he's having a hard time keeping up with his work because he was sick and got behind. I thank him for telling me that and ask what support he needs. He relaxes a little more. Suddenly we are relating in the field of friendship and we can explore going forward in a way that has feeling, shared context, and camaraderie.

Student-Teacher Conference:

Every interaction is a ceremony.

Be present.

Listen.

Open your senses.

Take in the student's whole presence.

Feel the river of energy—the natural wish to communicate.

{ Connection }

"Education is a social process; education is growth; education is not preparation for life, but is life itself."
—John Dewey[20]

The practice of friendship is not about always getting along. It's about staying in relationship, making our humanity available to our students and appreciating theirs. If we can relax and allow the doors of our heart and mind to be open, the world of others comes flooding in. Even if we feel distant from someone, we can open up on the spot and feel the hum of human connection that flows between us. We look at our student and take her in: the quality of her eyes, whether they make contact with ours or not, her posture, her clothing, and her habits. We feel something of her emotional state. We hear the quality of her voice, as well as the words she's conveying. At the end of our conversation, we may or may not have understood each other. Nonetheless, we have provided a space of relationship, which is true and good.

At times we may feel like we don't want to, or simply can't, be in relationship. Anger, fear, and preoccupation can shut down our hearts and minds. Being connected can feel too tender, intimate, and vivid. There's too much raw aliveness. Still, just as we develop trust in basic goodness through meditation, we can learn to return again and again to the practice of being in friendship. From there, we can invite others to join us, though we can never guarantee that they will. For some, the expression of genuineness—our native tongue—has become a foreign language. The best we can do is to keep speaking it, knowing that human beings are layered and that somewhere deep within, they recognize that genuine call and yearn to respond.

Here are a few stories about the experience of staying in relationship and holding trust in basic goodness.

Thien is an administrator at a high school in Madison, Wisconsin. One week she stepped in to break up a fight between two students and ended up getting hit really hard in the chest. She was rattled by the incident, both physically and emotionally. She spent a day crying on and off, feeling confused about what it means to be a teacher, but she decided not to press charges, and to be part of the student's readmit meeting after his suspension. She wanted to connect with him, to communicate with him. She wrote:

> He needs to claim and hold a message in his heart:
> he can LEARN from this. He can change from
> this. He can do better. This must be a message that
> I convey with my actions, words, and voice. I want
> to say very straightforwardly, if he does this again
> to someone else, he will not get a response like he
> got from me. He has to learn from this because if
> he doesn't, he will start down a path that will be

very dark. I BELIEVE in him. Our role as teachers has started to include physical danger. Every school year, we hear about staff that are hurt by students. I don't know what to do about this on a group level. I just know that I need this child to learn from this. I need to know that my pain and fear will be the fertile soil for this child to have a heartfelt learning experience.

After the meeting Thien wrote:

I spoke my truth. The student gave me eye contact and I could feel him listening. His facial expressions were open and he was present, he was empathizing. I ended my part by saying I would listen to anything he had to say. His mother prompted him to apologize and at that exact moment, I could see the shutter come down on his face. He was hardening against his heart, he did not want to feel anymore. Or maybe he could only feel and was not able to talk about it. He became glib and sarcastic. He refused to apologize. The decision was then made to send him home...I see him in the hallways and smile and say hello. He ignores me and looks the other way. I believe it's because I remind him of that moment his heart was soft. I don't know what he'll do next. His behavior has been less outrageous. This feels like a small triumph because I believe he REMEMBERS feeling.

Here is an experience of my own. Recently I had a student from Asia who had experienced a lot of violence in his previous schools and had gotten into trouble. I'll call him Joon. In desperation Joon's parents sent him abroad. By the time he came to my school he had lived in another Canadian province, which hadn't worked out. His English was pretty weak, and he presented as distant, shut down, and depressed. He was intensely attached to his smartphone, and retreated into its world at every opportunity. The week after he arrived at our school, his class went on a three-day trip to a nature awareness camp. We collected everyone's phones in order to have an unplugged experience of nature. Deep in the forest, surrounded by strangers, the last snow of winter, and the raw elements of fire, wind, water, and mud, Joon looked incredibly miserable. I could tell that full digital detox might really send him over the edge, so we let him keep his phone hidden away. Still, things were bad for him. He did only the minimum required of him, remained closed off to classmates, and sulked in a dark cloud. "Why did we come here?" he would say if encouraged to speak up, "It's so boring and pointless."

On the second day I decided to really lean into the Joon quagmire. I had no idea what to do for him, but I decided to practice friendship. I put myself in close proximity to him throughout the day. I talked with him here and there, asking about things, trying to understand through his accent and resistance to speaking up. Mostly I just stayed nearby so that I could interact in small ways.

Slowly Joon began to open up a little, which meant he became willing to complain to me about how unhappy he was. He also started telling me about his rough past, and he expressed some confused and judgmental views on his current situation. He was so happy to be away from violence, but he couldn't respect any of these kids, because they didn't fight—that sort of thing. He was trapped in a hellish realm of his own mind's creation. I wanted to correct some of his wrong ideas about the world and his situation, but I could tell that he'd had plenty of people telling him he was wrong. So I kept listening. I tried to stay in relationship, even though my heart and mind tended to flinch away from the trauma, aggression, and confusion that I could feel in the river that flowed there.

We did a lot of things to work with Joon and his situation. Over the next year things changed, but didn't improve much for him. He almost never spoke to anyone, but one day he came to sit with me in my classroom during a free period. He told me he was feeling terrible and that he thought he could talk to me. I realized the small gestures I had made to stay in relationship with him had created a thread of trust. I offered him a cookie, which he accepted and ate with no expression. While he sat he took out a pocketknife and a tiny black-and-white photograph of his mother. Carefully, almost ceremonially, he cut out the photo and taped it to a piece of paper. The sentiments he had expressed about his mother in the past had been harsh and resentful, but on this day he said he wanted to keep this picture around so that he could think about her. To me, it was like he was making a little shrine to basic goodness. I asked if his mom was ok, and he said she was fine, "but you never know what will happen in life." After he said this neither of us said anything for a while. The space felt sad and open as we chewed cookies and reflected on mothers, distance, and impermanence.

Then Joon spoke for a bit, telling me about his situation as he saw it. He showed great clarity about how he appeared to other people, about his longing for freedom from his destructive habits, his desire for friendship and love. But he was like a person in a whirlpool. He could see his predicament clearly, but he had no sense of faith that he could escape the momentum. He knew exactly what he needed to do. With effort he could swim to safety, but he lacked the will.

For me it was clear that Joon was a victim of the culture of separation. He presented as a fierce, independent, and violent youth, but his spirit was malnourished for lack of human connection. I worried about him a lot and spent time researching options for him, but a few weeks after our conversation, he was gone. His family had decided to bring him back home.

That was the end of my story with Joon. What do you think of it? It's not a success story. In fact, we failed to really bring him around, to instigate any academic breakthroughs for him, or to save him from his darkness. But somehow, across a gulf of separation, we made an ephemeral, human connection, and that felt meaningful. Who knows what will come of it?

In life, we can't measure or understand our efforts on the scale of effectiveness alone. Life is success and failure, good and bad, hot and cold. To practice true education we need to strive for success, but we also need to commit to honoring life and the social process that is society. As Parker Palmer said, "The tighter we cling to the norm of effectiveness the smaller the tasks we'll take on, because they are the only ones that get short-term results... Care about being effective, of course, but care even more about being faithful, as countless teachers do—faithful to your calling, and to the true needs of those entrusted to your care. You won't get the big jobs done in your lifetime, but if at the end of the day you can say, 'I was faithful,' I think you'll be okay."[21]

Teacher's Lounge:

Have a conversation with a colleague.

- ❖ Take turns sharing a story of a relationship you've had with a student that felt connected and alive.
- ❖ After hearing each story, reflect together: how did the teacher practice staying in relationship?
- ❖ Share another story about a relationship with a student that felt closed or disconnected.
- ❖ Reflect: what was getting in the way of being in relationship?

Discipline

Being a skillful disciplinarian is a form of mastery in teachers, but for many, discipline is among the least pleasant parts of teaching. If we teach because we like helping and connecting with young people, being the person who has to correct, remind, and reprimand them can sit uneasily with us. Discipline can feel like a fight, a constant struggle between the students' desire for freedom and our responsibility to maintain the learning environment. It can be aggravating, even infuriating, when students are disrespectful. It can be confusing, too: Sometimes we hear our own voice sounding a lot like a teacher we hated when we were young.

Part of what makes discipline challenging is that not many of us have had a positive relationship with it in our own lives. Discipline is usually experienced as something imposed on us by someone else or by ourselves. Often it has involved shame and intimidation—in some cases the threat of physical hurt, but more often the insinuation of banishment from the realm of belonging and approval.

While discipline is an integral aspect of a good learning environment, in a culture fraught with a feeling of unworthiness it can be problematic, reinforcing an underlying sense of badness.

But discipline can also be an expression of love and trust. It depends on the principle at the heart of the matter. Where is the discipline coming from, what is it in service to? Are we practicing discipline in service to basic goodness, or in service to fear?

Fear gives rise to aggression. When we're afraid, we try to get control. We want to crush the uncertainty that we feel, the vulnerability, so we go on the offensive. Shouting and cursing is one way that aggression shows up, but there are many others. Some of us have a sort of intellectual aggression—we like to bury our challengers under an avalanche of intelligence and credentials. Some of us have an aggression that fills up all the space with faux-cheerfulness and artificial laughter. Some of us have an oafish aggression—we listen, but without any intention of hearing. Some of us just whine and gossip around the copy machine. All of the ways we seek to avoid, destroy, or reinterpret the uncertainty and raw edges of our experience are forms of aggression.

What evokes our fear? For teachers it could be any number of things: a sense of losing control of our class; anticipation of looking foolish or being laughed at; defiance; feeling overwhelmed; being called out on our inadequacy; or not knowing what to do when something goes sideways in a discussion. Any of these situations can spark our fear and ignite our habitual aggression, our desire to keep hold of our territory. When our discipline comes from that place, it feels like a heavy lid coming down. Even if the message we're giving is a matter of common sense, aggressive discipline invites resistance. Our students feel like someone is puking an ego-trip on them.

In order to become a genuine disciplinarian, it's important to develop a disciplined relationship with ourselves to begin with. We can foster this in our meditation practice and in our daily activities. The key is to understand that discipline is not about punishment or endurance. It's a practice of loving ourselves. If we begin from basic goodness we don't use discipline to reinforce self-hatred. Rather, we use it to gently unravel the tangles of fear and aggression that are tied up in us. We practice discipline to call ourselves back again and again to our basic human goodness and to appreciate our existence.

Discipline can be as simple as sitting with a relaxed and upright posture, taking a moment to feel the natural dignity of our head and shoulders. Our haircut, our forehead, our eyeglasses, and our earrings are expressions of self-appreciation, which is discipline. Whether we have blue hair or receding hair doesn't matter. Discipline can be expanding and relaxing our shoulders like the wings of a bird, rather than slumping forward in overwhelm. Discipline can be resting our hands on our lap, releasing our tendency to fidget and fuss with our fingers, enjoying for a moment the simple goodness of our hands at rest. Discipline can be recognizing when we are caught in a habitual groove of distraction or irritation, and making an inner shift toward feeling the tenderness that underlies our thoughts. Speaking gently and truthfully is discipline, as is clowning it up when the situation calls for humor and levity. Discipline is not just following rules, but responding to living situations.

Discipline can also be expressed in our environment by washing our chalkboard at the end of the day, putting a flower in a glass, or straightening the chairs in the classroom—anything that communicates the feeling that "being here is worthwhile." A few years ago I went into the 3rd grade classroom when no one was there to steal a pencil from the teacher's desk and received a bit of a surprise. The inside of her desk was arranged with so much respect for every item—every notepad and paperclip. I was so impressed because no one, except the teacher and an occasional pencil thief, would be likely to see it. It reminded me of how Shibata Sensei, my Zen Archery teacher, had described one of the core disciplines of a warrior, "Taking care of every piece of equipment, no matter how small."

The real obstacle to practicing personal discipline is laziness. Generally, laziness means we don't want to work hard—we just want to flop and relax. But in this case, laziness means not wanting to feel. We don't want to touch the living energy of basic goodness. We don't want to feel the river of connection with others. We would prefer to be insulated and safe in our small zone of familiarity and control. This kind of laziness can show up as mild depression—a sort of murky, glum cloud that we inhabit. We prefer to slouch over our phone rather than sit up and connect with our environment. We prefer to dwell in daydreams rather than awakening into the present. On the other hand, our laziness might manifest as constant productivity. Keeping busy can be a great way to avoid feeling or opening to our whole experience. Discipline is developed as we begin to notice our personal favorite flavor of laziness. Recognizing our habits and style of neurosis allows us to work with them. Once again, gentleness is key. A big surge of effort just tires us out. Overcoming our laziness is accomplished through many small shifts in attitude, outlook, and action.

As we develop more appreciation for ourselves and our world, discipline begins to feel natural. We feel fully alive, which brings a natural clarity about what is helpful and what isn't. We feel uplifted. Therefore we cultivate what is healthy, gentle, and brilliant, and we let go of what is harmful, like aggression and laziness.

Having the personal discipline to work gently with ourselves gives us a basis for carrying out discipline in our classroom. We gain a sense of trust in ourselves, so we don't have to rely on aggression as power. Unclouded by our own fear and need for control, we can see our students' challenging behavior for what it is (often an expression of fear or pain) and respond accordingly. We use discipline to connect, to summon the inherent dignity in our students, and to foster an inspiring society.

Giving up aggression doesn't mean we have no strength. Sometimes we have to be the lion. If our students have turned into jackals, barking and biting, we may roar to turn them back into lion cubs. We can absolutely be fierce, ferocious even, without aggression. Then when the situation changes we can drop it. If we're not just losing our temper, the discipline feels clean, and we can carry on without resentment.

If the teacher has a sense of natural ease and appreciation that she expresses in her personal discipline and classroom discipline, the students can tune into that. Rather than feeling oppressed, they feel invited into the spirit of the discipline, which is caring for themselves and their world.

Teacher Rules:

Reflect:

- ❖ What does discipline feel like in your school?
- ❖ What does it feel like in your classroom?
- ❖ Do you notice fear coming up in your teaching life?

❖ Do you recognize aggression or laziness in your way of relating to yourself, your job, or your students?

❖ What does aggression feel like?

❖ What does laziness feel like?

Practice discipline:

❖ By opening to basic goodness in each moment

❖ By letting go of aggression and laziness in each moment

❖ By cultivating gentleness in yourself and toward yourself

❖ As a continuous process, not an ideal to live up to

Use discipline:

❖ To teach

❖ To connect

❖ To protect

❖ To calm

Avoid using discipline:

❖ To punish

❖ To shame

❖ To overpower

{ Kindling the Hearth }

I'm watching three 2nd grade girls play a game with a deck of cards that have puppy and kitten pictures on them. The game does not seem to have any rules or objective—they're making it up as they go. As they giggle and discuss, they glance up at each other occasionally. One girl announces that she's making a "cuteness corner," but the others object for some reason so she requests to be "the mom," and they say fine. After a while one of the girls gets upset and storms off, but she comes back about thirty seconds later and reintegrates. In this way, the girls both play and learn, making meaning of their experience as they interact. As human beings we attune ourselves to the messages in our environment.[22] If the message is warm, we attune our hearts in that direction. If the message is hostile and fearful, we attune our hearts that way.

Sometimes we think our small gestures, greetings, and exchanges are insignificant, but they all help weave a culture, which becomes profoundly meaningful. Vaughan Doucette, an elder of the Eskasoni Mi'kmaw community, wrote this after visiting the school where I teach.

From the time I went to Kindergarten to the time I went to school off Reserve I was bullied every day. Over the years I was struck so many times in the head that my head is scarred still today. I bring this up to show a contrast that I experienced during my last visit to your beautiful school. At the beginning of the day I witnessed something that I never saw before in my experience as a child in school...that was the kindness of the teachers. The simple act of greeting each child as they came and left was so moving for me. I was moved to tears when I saw the children being so lovingly taught and cared for.[23]

That kind of warmth is essential, but in order to have warmth we need fire. For so much of history, cultures have been built around hearth fires. Sitting around the wood stove or the fire pit people have told and listened to stories, cooked food and made tea, laughed, talked, and sung songs. Today, despite our amazing new ways of communicating, human togetherness has become scarce. As wonderful as the computer is, it's a cold hearth to gather around, and doesn't plug us into the energy of social goodness. As educators it's important that we find creative ways to rekindle the hearth of natural connection. We can do this by learning to create safe spaces, facilitating real conversations and telling stories. We can find ways to enjoy food together, even lighting a candle or putting flowers on the table. We can work to foster the arts, not just as one subject among other subjects, but as a way of binding our communities through emotion and beauty.

If nothing else, we can be kind. Kindness is the spark that will restore life to the world, the underlying principle of an ethical society, the one true ember that we need to pass on to the young. Creating a culture of kindness is not just a matter of playing nicely with others. It's an epic project of personal, educational, and social transformation. It will often mean standing against the rushing currents of individualism, blame, and business-as-usual. In order to truly be kind, we need bravery.

PART IV: TEACHING LIKE THE SUN

Just as the sun illuminates and warms the earth, the brave teacher inspires vision and growth.

{ Bravery }

When I was becoming a parent for the first time, I was pretty scared. I definitely did not feel ready. I do know a few people who truly seemed to have their acts together before having children—stable career, established marriage, good house, and so on—but for most of my friends (and myself) there was a feeling of leaping off a cliff without a parachute. My friend Alexandra, who was younger than me and already had a beautiful son, shared some advice that really helped me. She said that in her mind it was good that her children would see her continue to grow up, to face challenges, to learn and make mistakes, even as she was helping them to grow up and learn to be in this world. We often think that as adults we are supposed to be finished products. We think we should appear godlike to young people, like Poseidon or Athena, but in truth we often feel like overgrown children masquerading as grownups. We've grown up with the idea that at some point we will get over the ridge that we're climbing and then we'll be able to coast. We will have *arrived*. But somehow we never quite get there. We never come to the end of our challenges. At the crest of each hill we may see a downhill run, but we soon catch a glimpse of another peak rising before us. The discovery of real wisdom is often less glorious than the myth we've been dreaming of. It's more about relaxing into the journey and less about arriving at a destination. It might feel like a let-down, but our journey is made up of challenges. Endless challenges. This is good news for teachers. Since young people face continuous challenges (including some created by us), it's appropriate that we have challenges too. Living in the challenge makes us human.

In the Shambhala tradition, challenges are regarded as the dignity of one's life. Rather than seeing challenges as "one goddamn thing after another," we begin to see them as natural energy. This isn't about finding a personal advantage in situations the way some business leadership books and personal training programs advise. In life and in education, winning, selling, and making a profit don't always make a healthy central motive. Let's begin by accepting that challenges are an inevitable result of life activity. As we live and grow and try to work with others, we experience constant change and discord—challenges as complex as huge community upsets, or as simple as sour milk in our tea. Lice outbreak? Angry parents? Paperwork? Fidget-spinners? There's always something. To the extent that we've invested our hopes and fears in a particular outcome, we will be distraught when something else happens. From habit we either fight harder and harder to make things work out the way we want them to, or we give up and shield ourselves with a cynical attitude: "Oh well, it's all pointless anyhow...."

If we approach life situations with an attitude of worthiness, and we cultivate trust, care, and vulnerability in our beings, it's possible to see challenges more accurately. Rather than automatically taking situations as personal attacks, we have more room to view them holistically. Seeing past the surface level of the story, we can explore its energetic qualities. Rather than solidifying around our first impression, we can allow space. Then situations have a chance to bloom and reveal themselves more fully. Challenges are valuable sources of information—they give us continuous messages. Whether we respond to those messages with habitual fear and aggression or with inquisitiveness and compassionate skill will depend on our bravery in the moment.

Bravery is the key to living and teaching with goodness in the midst of challenge. We need to acknowledge that challenges exist and will always arise, and we also must be able to move forward. We can't let challenges define us or overrun us. We need to be able to live *forward*, toward growth, love, and awakening, which is very difficult to do with a small mind. Acknowledging that those challenges are there and moving forward anyways takes a big mind and a big heart. That's bravery. Rather than shutting down in tough moments, we can learn to relax into the greater space of basic goodness. A small mind is quickly overwhelmed. With a big mind and heart, we have the capacity to accommodate all kinds of situations. We may not know what to do, but we maintain a sense of possibility even when things seem impossible. Difficulty can make us shrink and feel limited or cornered. With the bravery of basic goodness, our minds and hearts are like the open sky, and situations are like the weather that plays and dances within it.

Just being a teacher at all takes a certain level of bravery. Sometimes we forget how amazing it is that we are able to walk into our classrooms and do what we do. If you are a teacher now, do you remember your first day? Somehow you were able to open your mind and heart enough to accommodate the fear you felt and, at least to some extent, to meet the "weather" that was your students in all of their terrifying glory. But to hold such fickle and vibrant energy day-to-day and moment-to-moment, without shutting down and reverting to old, narrow pathways, takes practice. In the next chapters I'll offer some ways of reconnecting with our innate bravery—even in the midst of everyday challenges, great and small.

Backpack Check:

Take a few minutes to consider and acknowledge your challenges. Begin by sitting for a minute and taking a deep breath. Then bring to mind and gently survey the difficult parts of your teaching practice. For now, don't attempt to problem solve. Just feel the textures of the challenges that are there, as if you were feeling the shapes of rocks in a backpack. Often, they will be of two varieties:

1. Sharp—obstacles that sting, pierce, or agitate us. Situations that feel worrisome, stressful, or painful—the sort that might keep us awake at night.
2. Smooth—obstacles that are less obvious, but still weigh on us. For example, we might be good at our jobs, but feel a lack of connection with our students, or we might just have a vague feeling that some greater vitality is possible in our work, but we don't know how to find it.

As you feel the textures of each challenge, journal some adjectives and images that arise. For example, you might write, "Chunky, pulsing, red," for one obstacle, and "Watery, elusive, cold," for another.

{ Surrender }

Sometimes when we get overwhelmed it can feel like we can't breathe. We may even literally forget to breathe. The first step toward bravery, the first breath of fresh air, is surrender. This is probably not the first word that comes to mind when you think of your brave heroes, whomever they may be, and yet it is intimacy with surrender that allows authentic heroes to rise above a mere show of personality, to somehow embody a depth of love and power that is bigger than life.

Surrender in this context does not mean giving up. Giving up is a result of frustration and a feeling of not having the capacity to stay engaged. The moments when teachers give up on students or themselves are very sad ones. Surrender, on the other hand, is a process of letting go of our small mind, our personalized plan, our desire to control our world. If we want to work with our challenges, we have to begin by acknowledging them. This sounds obvious, but how often, out of pride or fear, do we try to get around this crucial step? If we know exactly how to handle a situation, it's not a challenge. Therefore, challenges are situations that we don't fully know how to handle. Having the humility to acknowledge this is the tender birthplace of real bravery. We are not running away, but are willing to remain in the midst of uncertainty.

We all possess a great resource, a treasury of wisdom, love, and energy that is available to us as human beings. Teachers are often eager to embrace new methods, technologies, curriculums, or techniques that can help us help our students. This is good, and there are a great many excellent methods that can help us. But still, in order to practice them with authenticity, to teach with authenticity, we have to be who we are. We are not just a bundle of lesson plans, policies, and best practices. All of those things can be tools at our command, but they shouldn't be the shield we use to cover our genuine selves. Surrender is dropping our shield—dissolving our resistance to being human, with all of its uncertainty. When we surrender we find that our capacity is greater than we imagined, and our ability to be pragmatic in response to situations becomes very sharp.

What are we surrendering to? We are surrendering to reality. When we say human beings possess wisdom, it means we have the ability to know reality. Therefore, rather than only dwelling in our run-down little hut of ideas, we can open ourselves to the reality of things as they are. When we do so, we discover possibilities and energy that we didn't previously see or feel. It's like coming out of our little hut, breathing the fresh air and seeing a big sky full of stars. This is similar to the feeling we might have when getting ready to perform on stage: Part of us wants to hide, to hang on to our safety, but when we surrender to the reality of the performance we feel totally alive.

One of my idols growing up was a man named Will Ryken. Will's combination of gentleness and fierceness inspired hundreds of young people who came to a unique camp that he led called Shambhala Sun Summer Camp. The camp consisted of just one week living in tents in the mountains each year, but for many of us it became a pivotal experience. Will's presence was a big part of it. Above all, there was a sense of his complete surrender to us—the campers—and to the environment—the sun, wind, rain, fire, and earth. Will created a unique feeling of love and challenge. At camp we felt totally worthy, and at the same time, we had something big to live up to.

When I got older I staffed Sun Camp and eventually became one of its leaders. For those of us who took over the leadership, there was some trepidation about living up to Will's example. I dearly wanted to be as big-hearted and powerful a leader as he was, but I wasn't sure I knew how, and I struggled with this in the back of my mind as I led my first few camps. One year, toward the end of a camp that I was leading, I got some help. I had worked hard to arrange things for a strong ending in the last days of camp, including handing over a lot of responsibility to the teenage leaders within the camp. I had big plans for the second-to-last day's activities, ceremonies, and feast, but that morning I woke up with a shock when a huge thunderclap shook the valley. It was barely sun up when a massive storm broke. Rain began slashing down so hard that tents were falling over and lightning was flashing all around. I ran to some of the collapsed tents and picked up their walls to look at the children huddled within as rainwater gushed off the sides. Suddenly I had a feeling of dizziness—a total loss of control. I didn't know what to do or what to think. Not only were my plans washing away in the downpour, the camp itself—my responsibility—was getting flattened by a force that was vastly superior to my will. For a moment I felt panic rising as I tried to get my bearings. And then I noticed that I was standing in an open field, holding a metal tent pole, in the middle of a lightning storm. I had to give up. I put the pole down and took shelter. A little while later, the rain stopped and the sun came out. Everyone emerged from their tents and all sorts of things started to happen. There was a sense of exhilaration and joy in the camp. As the morning sun warmed up the earth, steam rose from the wet clothing that the children were wearing. The teenage leaders started fixing tents and getting things organized. Some of them, having completely surrendered to the wet, were gleefully sliding down the wet grass of the hill on their stomachs. I realized that what was happening was real, living, and dynamic. My plans and sense of control were crushed like a paper cup, and yet I felt totally liberated and energized.

Opening through surrender into bravery doesn't need to be as dramatic as that experience. In fact, we do it all the time. We just let go and work with what's happening instead of forcing it. Whenever we recognize resistance, either in ourselves or in our students, we have the opportunity to create space. If we let go of our preoccupation, more space becomes available in which we can see what's happening. When our students seem distracted and out of it we might get really frustrated. We might get angry with them or disappointed in ourselves. But we could also recall that there is a message in the resistance, beckoning us to look more deeply. We could let go for a moment and feel what's happening. Then we might notice things we hadn't seen before. Maybe we notice that some of our students aren't looking at each other—there's been an argument and the vibes are making them uncomfortable. Or maybe it's early spring and the sunshine is seducing everyone's spirits out the windows. Or maybe we didn't explain something clearly. Or maybe they're just out of it and we don't know why. We don't always have to solve the problem. There may not even be a problem! But letting go, returning to a sense of reality in this moment, allows us to work with the situation in a more connected way. It's like taking off our work gloves—with our bare hands we can feel more.

Surrender can feel scary. It can mean not knowing what to do, or what will happen in the next moment. That feeling of uncertainty is abhorrent to the part of our mind that is addicted to control. In order to be brave in uncertainty we need to have trust that the open space of our experience is our own basic goodness. We are the sky—so there's no need to be afraid of falling into the deep, open blue. Trusting ourselves in this way, even just a little bit, allows us to accommodate energy and chaos in our classroom. Sometimes we can even play with it.

Try This:

- ❖ **Recognize resistance.** Notice when you feel challenged. Feel the quality of wanting things to be different than they are, or when people or situations are pushing against your agenda.
- ❖ **Let go of the desire to control the situation**. Return to the present. Connect with your body, senses, and environment.
- ❖ **Rest with uncertainty.** Don't leap to fix or escape. Feel.
- ❖ **Listen.** Invite intuition. Allow a fuller picture to emerge.

{ Vision }

Having taken a breath and surrendered to the situation as it is, we can move forward. But where are we going? In order to bravely meet the challenges of teaching and move forward each year with inspiration and genuineness, it is essential to have a sense of vision. Vision gives us depth and sustainability. It works closely with our sense of motivation, which we explored earlier. Motivation, like fuel, is very immediate—it's where we are coming from right now. Vision is a broader perspective—it's about where we are going. Many people teach for a year or two riding the bronco of ambition, and then either get bored or burn out. Others can teach for decades without heart, like a broken mule, repeating dusty old lesson plans and even telling the same jokes on the same days each year. But teachers who know how to engage their classes, to stay alive in their subjects, and to care for the whole life of their teaching experience, have vision.

Why is teaching worth it to you?

What sort of world do you want to bring into being?

What sort of human beings do you want to help train?

When you ponder these questions you are exploring the territory of vision. What is your vision for education? What's your biggest idea? Having a sense of vision infuses meaning and purpose into our activity. It helps us to avoid getting lost in the minutia of our day-to-day work—to hold a bigger perspective. It also helps us to avoid getting lost in our own moods—the ups and downs of our job. Sometimes we love our work and other times we hate it. The vital factor that guides us beyond these ups and downs is to have a true sense of what we are working for.

To explore this, we can reflect on a question like one of those above, or another question like, "Why do I teach?" We should choose a question that doesn't have an immediate answer, but invokes some depth of reflection. Let the question sit in your mind and settle into your body. It's not an interrogation, but an opportunity for honest and gentle self-reflection. Notice what feelings, uncertainties, and answers arise. Then ask the question again. Each time, expand the focus of your inquiry. For example:

Why do I teach? (How does it nourish me?)
Why do I teach? (What do I want to give my students?)
Why do I teach? (How do I hope this work will influence society?)

Finding our way to the heart of these questions can lead us to the discovery of a more personal sense of vision. We may have words for what we find, or just feelings. We may only find wonder or uncertainty. In any case, by contemplating the questions we begin to look beyond ourselves and our own short-term needs. Our minds are nourished when they look to something bigger than us. Some people can work just for money, but not teachers. Teachers don't usually get paid very well anyway and, more to the point, our work is too important to be motivated by self-serving ends alone.

We need to think bigger. We are weaving the fabric of society for the lives of young people now and in the future. Having vision is like placing the sun in our own sky. It raises our gaze from our feet to the horizon. It gives us orientation.

When we begin to feel the energy of vision in our lives, we may be faced with a few challenges, or reactions, that can come up in our own minds as well as from others. The first one is fear. We may feel that this big vision belittles us. We are afraid that we can't live up to it. We feel that it's too much for us—it's too much work, there's too much to learn, and it's just too big to handle. So we want to lower the bar, to make the vision smaller and more manageable. At the same time we may feel afraid of being left out. The vision is compelling and meaningful but we feel afraid that we won't have enough to offer. We're afraid that we can't control it or direct it. So we want to keep it private—we get stingy with our vision and scheme about ways to trademark and sell it.

Another reaction that vision provokes is the accusation of naïveté. This is the voice of the cynic that rises up to kick vision off its horse. If we bring up basic goodness or compassion sometimes people feel compelled to push back, calling these simple-minded ideals and promoting so-called pragmatism in the form of justified aggression or economic bottom lines.

Of course, we should contemplate our doubts. Having vision, having the sun in our sky, is not meant to belittle or embarrass us. It's not meant to make us feel inadequate, to feel like our own vision gives us one more thing that we can't live up to. We're not actually supposed to reach the sun. We're supposed to allow the sun to illuminate our life and give us warmth. The purpose of having vision is to be nourished and strengthened and to find clarity. Therefore, we have to be brave enough to hold our vision, and we have to feel worthy of it. How we think and feel about our role is important. We should not only think of ourselves as babysitters and paper graders with mediocre paychecks. We should think of our role with a sense of dignity and sacredness. As teachers we are healers, protectors, elders, artists, activists, and illuminators. At least we can give ourselves that much! We can have a sense of poetry in our life and offer our work that kind of blessing and empowerment.

We have to test our vision with critical inquiry. But these days we need to beware the impulsive voice of the cynic, which is a voice of laziness more than clarity. It's easy to tear things down, to criticize and belittle them from the safety of our own smug intellectualism. This can be a real shadow in the world of academia. Still, there is a difference between having a sense of vision and distracting ourselves with a pleasant dream. A genuine vision for positive transformation doesn't ignore the reality of where we are now. Rather than being cynical, we can use our sharp, critical mind to keep ourselves grounded even as we expand our sense of possibility.

When we have that clarity of vision we engage in our activities in a detailed manner. We can be satisfied with small actions. We know the scope of our vision as well as the tangles and challenges of our work, and we are happy to take small steps forward. We work with the details of our daily tasks and we feel content. On the other hand, when our work lacks vision we lose perspective and inspiration and we just work to get by.

If we're teaching young people and our motivation is just to get by, what kind of vision are we serving? Most likely it's the vision of the status quo, which may seem neutral but is generally imbued with the values of "imperialist white supremacist capitalist patriarchy," to borrow bell hooks' powerful phrase. If we wish to practice an education that promotes other values we need the bravery of vision.

This doesn't mean we necessarily need to have a political agenda. My stepfather Mike ran a coffee shop for over thirty years and he was a visionary. For him, work wasn't just about profit. Everyone who came and worked in the coffee shop soon found out that something different was going on there. It felt more meaningful than they'd expected it to. Mike wouldn't spell out his vision for them with words, but he embodied it. Someone would get hired for a job washing dishes and in the back of their mind would be thinking it was a demeaning job and would feel resentful and low about it. But Mike had real respect for people. He felt that the time people gave to work was a part of their life, which was sacred, and therefore the activities filling that time were worthy of respect. He would show them how to wash dishes, not only fast and well, but with dignity and respect for themselves. For some people, this approach felt too intimate and revealing. They didn't want to learn a whole new approach to life—they just wanted a stupid job. Some quit, but others saw Mike as a mentor. They began to intuit his vision and to feel inspired that it could be expressed in such an ordinary way.

Gardening Class:

Sky:

Contemplate your vision for teaching. Find a question that is powerful for you. You can use the questions offered in this chapter, or, if you like, spend some time crafting a powerful question of your own. A powerful question leads you to the heart of things—that place of expansive, forward energy. Think big. Don't get caught up in practicalities or cynicism. This is about purpose. Contemplate inwardly, or by journaling, or through conversation with a colleague.

Earth:

Having contemplated your vast vision, allow the rain and sun to nourish the earth. Consider any aspect of your teaching life and contemplate how it can grow toward your vision. Think about things like: how you feel when you go to work; how your classroom feels and is set up; how you interact with your students; how your lessons affect the culture; the students' experience of school life, or of your class; the color of ink you use to mark papers; and so on. Consider the daily ceremonies of your school life. Don't try to take it all on at once. Pick one or two areas and contemplate, "Does this reflect and serve my vision?" If it does, enjoy that feeling. If not, consider how it might change, adapt, or grow. Think small. Not small in a petty way, but in a pragmatic way: What actual step can you take to move forward? Some steps are tiny, some are bold. Be content to see these sprouts of action growing toward the sun.

Cleverness

"If you maintain a sense of humor, and a distrust of the rules laid down around you, there will be success." –Chögyam Trungpa

When you have vision, then you have something worthy to serve. It's like knowing who your true boss is. You have a secret boss and you're a secret agent. You may have a boss at work, but you actually work for something else, which is your vision. We need this, because otherwise we can only live up to our boss' vision, or the system's vision. We may feel like we have big ideas, but we're not allowed to explore them. The parameters of our job can be so narrow that having a vision can seem pointless. We may have to work within the confines of our situation, but we still need to have vision, even if it's our secret. This is the kind of secret that gives us strength.

With the strength of bravery we find ways to move forward. Sometimes that means going around an obstacle rather than through it. There's an old story of a Taoist master who comes to a place where a skittish horse keeps kicking everyone who tries to walk down the street. What does the master do? She walks down a different street.

When we know what we are truly working toward we don't get as mesmerized by the obstacles that come up. We have more fun and we become more creative.

Genuine bravery arises from a mind that is relaxed and appreciates its own expansive nature. Through meditation practice we develop some familiarity with the open quality of our being. We learn how to let go of thoughts, and in the process we become less absorbed in them. We learn that thoughts are less like iron and more like mist. This gives us a sense of humor about ourselves. We begin to see that our personal problems have been exacerbated by our thoughts. We tend to complicate matters immensely by viewing them solely through the lens of tight thinking and rigid concepts. When we let go of this entrapment we feel more open and relaxed. We gain clarity and can relate to situations in a more matter-of-fact way. At the same time, our experience of the ephemeral quality of our own thoughts allows us to have some healthy skepticism toward social challenges, which themselves are the result of many people's thoughts. Thus, we begin to feel open to possibilities of a more flexible and clever approach to seemingly inflexible situations.

Sometimes teacher and parent communities are filled with scheming and gossip. Cleverness in this case does not mean getting embroiled in all that. Nor is it about finding shortcuts to avoid hard work, or cheap tricks for getting our own way. Here we are talking about having the bravery to hold true to our vision. If we long to create a natural and kind culture in our classroom, school, and community, and to rediscover the magical heart of learning in education, we will need to be creative and intelligent. Even thinking this way takes bravery. Taking steps to make it real often means going against the grain because, to a greater or lesser extent, we are all embroiled in the systems and habits of our culture. Getting on our high horse and charging into the mess usually just alienates others and wears us out. So the notion of cleverness is about finding ways to move forward skillfully, especially in difficult situations.

The first step is to find our own strength, which is the energy arising from basic goodness. That genuine mind and heart is our ground. From that foundation we have a sense of inner victory. We are already good, so we can afford to be open and generous with whatever we meet. We don't see our day as a business deal in which we will only find satisfaction if the world meets our hopes and expectations. As the ancient Chinese strategist Sun Tzu wrote, "The fight is chaotic yet one is not subject to chaos... One's form is round and one cannot be defeated."[24] If we enter the classroom brittle and irritable, it's likely that our students will break us. Beginning from strength does not mean we set our jaw, harden our heart, and go in ready to fight. It means we touch our genuineness. We may feel tender and uncertain, but that does not make us weak. "One's form is round"—our being is whole, worthy, and good, like a circle, which is open but can't be broken.

That genuine, open quality of our being gives us strength because we don't have to defend it. From openness, we can get right into things. We don't remain aloof in our goodness. We get right into the work of being with our students, utilizing all the skills we have mustered. We make mistakes all the time, which makes us more curious. We ask, "How do we *not* get kicked by the same horse next time?" Like a clever strategist, obstacles perk our creativity. Like a good math student navigating a tricky problem, we hold steady when it gets difficult, and remain alert as we look for the solution. We look for openings—cracks in the system that let us teach more vibrantly, cracks in our students' armor that let us encourage their genuineness. If we work in a den of gossip and negativity, we find ways to practice good speech. We take a fierce stand for things that are worth it, and practice patience with those that are immovable for now.

We certainly don't always feel clever. Sometimes we're just confused. But we should have the bravery of knowing that our natural sensibility will help us. We do possess intelligence and kindness— the resources we need. They are always churning up within our senses, our bodies, and our experience. When we're mixed up, we might just want to listen for a while. Go back to surrender. Go back to vision. Listen to the whole situation. Be awake. And when you suddenly know what to do, remember to enjoy it.

Game Plan:

First, Win:

Creativity and cleverness arise from an open and relaxed mind, which in turn arises from trust in basic goodness. We develop trust through regular meditation practice. Don't try to solve your problems by meditating, but meditate genuinely, as you are, and connect with the unbroken human goodness that precedes thoughts. From here, problems are seen for what they truly are, free of the filters of hope and fear.

Then, Play:

Regard difficult situations as reminders to activate curiosity.

Maintain a sense of humor. Situations are created by thoughts. Thoughts are like mist. Don't be so convinced of their solidity.

Distrust the rules laid down around you. If the prescribed pathways are fraught with peril, consider going another way.

Expand your knowledge.

- ❖ Develop your skills and knowledge. There are countless methodologies and best practices, but don't make them ends in themselves. Use them as tools to serve your vision.
- ❖ Bring in more perspectives. Share your thoughts and challenges with friends and colleagues. Have creative and dignified conversations—avoid complaining.
- ❖ To learn even more about skillfulness and cleverness, study *The Art of War* by Sun Tzu.[25]

Invite your deeper intelligence.

- ❖ Confucius used to consult the sages in his dreams. Why not invite the sages to visit your dreams? If they come, ask for advice.
- ❖ If you're trying to untangle a complicated issue, try making art. Art activates dimensions of mind and heart that can help us perceive things in a new way and unleash fresh insights.
- ❖ Consider timing. Everything is always in flux. Do you need to act swiftly? Sometimes a situation simply needs time to ripen and will sort itself out or reveal a new opportunity.

{ Teaching the Sky }

"It's who you serve that determines the quality of your being." —bell hooks[26]

Another practice of bravery is to maintain a virtuous outlook. In Shambhala this is called practicing the view. We are learning to remember and recognize the innate goodness in our students, no matter how they act or present themselves. Some students are quick and responsive; some are suspicious and disinterested. Some are sweet and some are angry. Some students love to learn; others are dead set against it. Some are privileged and some are marginalized. Skater kids, country kids, rich or poor, boys, girls, gender non-binary, geeks, nerds, jocks, goths, and so on. The view is that each one is like the sky.

What are the qualities of the sky? It is vast and beautiful. Just so, each student possesses a quality of being that is open, innocent, and fathomless. Each has a capacity for expressing genuine beauty and connection.

The sky is also a playground for all kinds of weather, and young people are full of weather. Sometimes there are storms, and sometimes the sky is overcast and grey. At times the clouds may seem so solid that we can't believe the sky could ever be blue—in the same way, we all experience confusion and darkness. We have to remember that our students don't know themselves. They don't know their own blue skies, and they are alternately fascinated by, confused by, and tortured by their own clouds. Knowing this, we have compassion for them. Holding the view is trusting that the sky is still blue, even when it's full of clouds. We see our students as fundamentally good, regardless of how they behave.

Finally, the sky is dynamic and alive. It's constantly changing, full of energy and unpredictability. I've spent a lot of time in the mountains of Colorado, where summer skies can unleash sudden hailstorms, and give way moments later to blazing sunshine and rainbows. Young people too are like this—insolent one moment, innocent the next. Sunshine and patches of blue are constantly breaking through like smiles; the winds of fear and insecurity are constantly blowing into the clouds of distraction, fixation, and laziness. Our ability to work with the weather, responding to it in each moment, comes from a ground of trust and care born of working with our own experience. A single student or an entire class can shift on a dime. Minds suddenly open. Emotions suddenly well up. Can we be free enough of our own prejudice and fixed mind to dance with the energy in the moment?

Holding the view of basic goodness comes down to being genuine, and seeing the genuineness in our students. It makes us soft, because a genuine person is warm and natural. On the other hand, it makes us sharp, because we are looking for genuineness in our students, and we don't buy into fakeness. It's not easy to keep this view all the time—we have to practice strengthening it through meditation and contemplation. It helps to reflect on how basic goodness is revealed in our students. One way we have of doing this, which is common to many teachers who find joy and love in being with young people, has been described as "appreciating shining moments." We take delight in the moments when our students display their unvarnished goodness—a moment of pure tenderness, a flash of discovery, an accidental expression of genius, a gesture of kindness, a child's face in a moment of quiet reflection. Goodness is always bubbling up. Joaquin was a 12-year-old boy I taught who had a very low affect, seeming to show almost no emotion or care about anything. It was a little disconcerting to interact with him; he seemed almost robotic, and I wondered if I could find that genuine spot in him. One morning though, I watched him escort his little sister to her classroom. As she took off her coat and backpack Joaquin helped her with great care. It reminded me of an old butler attending his master. There was a feeling of natural duty, familiarity, and quiet affection as, without a word, he held her mittens, helped her unbutton her coat, hung them both neatly on her hook, and handed over her lunchbox.

Appreciating these shining, human moments can inspire and remind us that goodness is still alive. But holding the view of goodness when people act badly is more difficult. A true understanding of basic goodness includes knowing that clouds and storms are all part of the sky. We can have compassion for people who are caught in the storms of their own self-doubt. We should know that people suffer when they don't trust and express their true nature. Young people suffer from the confusion of growing up and not trusting themselves. Not knowing oneself to be good is like having a wound.

It makes us fearful. It can make us paranoid of others, angry, morose, or desperate. Acting out, underachieving, bullying, self-harm, drug abuse, and so on all begin there. Every nasty remark or act of aggression has many layers of motivation—we can't always figure out why people do what they do, but we can know that at the root there is that wound, that basic lack of self-love. Having compassion means knowing that everyone's actions have a context. It means caring for the suffering of everyone, not only those who seem to deserve it.

This means we can never condemn anyone. We can't just be done with them or see them as monsters. Sometimes when a child does something wrong in school there is a sort of kerfuffle of papers and policies as the faculty applies its pre-formulated response. Discipline policies and prescribed consequences are important: They provide a backbone for the school to work with a range of scenarios, and sometimes they have something to teach the child. But they are not an answer to pain. Compassion is an answer to pain. Holding the view means knowing that wherever we witness aggression or confusion there is pain, and wherever there is pain there is original goodness unrecognized.

Compassion doesn't mean we just have to be nice, and hand out affirmations all the time. It takes guts and an open heart to look at situations and consider what is truly beneficial to each student and to the whole. We may have to expel a child, or we may have to stand up for a student in a staff meeting. Holding bravery, compassion, and basic goodness may sound like a balancing act, but actually these qualities come from relaxation. Just as the sun gives warmth and light, we can shine out naturally into our lives.

At this time when so much confusion and darkness come out of the feeling of badness, we can make a big difference in the lives of young people. By seeing them with the eyes of goodness, we may be the only reference point they have of something true and kind. Will they recognize and appreciate it? Maybe so, maybe not. Either way, it's a great blessing to offer and it will benefit us as well as them.

Teachers Also Have Eyes on the Front of Their Heads

Practice the Bravery of the View:

* ❖ **Touch basic goodness and radiate it out like the sun**. Accept and include all students in the view of this natural understanding. Practice doing this again and again.
* ❖ **Appreciate shining moments**. For a week or two, keep a shining moments journal. Each day write down at least one moment when a student's natural goodness manifested itself. If a group of colleagues does this together, you can share them at the end of the week.
* ❖ **Be compassionate.** Know that everyone struggles and everyone suffers. Even negative and harmful behavior is a confused attempt to rediscover goodness. Radiate warmth from your heart.
* ❖ **Reflect the goodness you see.** Without being pretentious or overly precious, find ways to bless and acknowledge the brilliance, kindness, dignity, tenderness, and joy that come forth from your students as natural expressions of their inherent nobility.

PART V: TOUCHING THE EARTH

In each moment we can touch
the earth, honoring the depth
and poignancy of our ordinary
experience. Progress along
the path comes more from
recognizing and appreciating
where we are than from
aiming for a destination.

Simplicity

The inner path of the teacher progresses in a natural way, like the growth of a child. While the child's body grows in a linear fashion, her inner life unfolds in cycles, opening to new worlds of learning and discovery only when her body and mind have gained the nourishment they need to do so. If we push a child beyond the level she is ready for, she may rise to the occasion, but not without sacrificing some of the learning she was still absorbing. Eventually, in order to be strong and healthy, she may have to go back and complete those earlier lessons. Our path as teachers who aspire to embody genuineness, kindness, and bravery in the classroom, is a journey that opens outward, moving from small and fearful minds to radiant and joyful ways of being. Yet this journey is not like a trek across a desert or a hike to the peak of a mountain. It's more like growing up, experiencing life through the seasons. As we grow older we can either become more stingy and embedded in our habits, or we can grow more free and available to others. The difference lies in how we have learned to work with our minds and our experience. To the degree that we have learned to be genuine with ourselves we will be able to foster genuineness in the classroom.

Master teachers can read the signs of development in their students, knowing when they are ready to be brought along to the next stage of learning. In Chögyam Trungpa's writing there is a beautiful description of the learning journey from fear to bravery called *The Education of the Warrior.* I've referenced some of the images from this passage a few times in this book. Now we'll walk through each of its stages, which offer us an overview of the landscape and appreciation for the journey. We are the ones who have access to our own inner life, so while we can be supported by teachers and friends along the way, it's up to us to read the signs of our own development and move forward to each new stage of growth. *The Education of the Warrior* begins:

> *That mind of fearfulness*
> *Should be put in the cradle of loving-kindness*
> *And suckled with the profound and brilliant milk of eternal doubtlessness*
> *In the cool shade of fearlessness, fan it with the fan of joy and happiness.*

Fearlessness, loving-kindness, doubtlessness, joy, and happiness are the supports for relaxing into the basic simplicity of being human. Our fearful minds are full of self-doubt, which makes us unhappy, fixated, and aggressive. In young children it's kind of cute, but grown up fear is often less charming, more sophisticated, and sometimes quite nasty in its expression. Nevertheless, no matter how old or seemingly complicated we are, we need the basic nourishment of trust and care so that we can learn to simply be, which is the root of peace.

Having a taste for the goodness of our own being is the foundation for supporting others. To a greater or lesser degree our students are wrapped in the habits of fearfulness, but we can offer them the conditions they need to emerge as their genuine selves. We can teach knowing that our students *are* good, therefore they can learn to *be* good. If we teach with the approach that our students are not good, but could become good, we're trying to change them into an ideal that only lives in our concepts. Thus we layer in the base of fear.

Even loving and skilled teachers often use fear and intimidation as ways to motivate students to perform and behave. We want them to do their homework so we make them feel bad about not doing it. We train them to dread the shame of showing up empty-handed. Teachers create a scale of approval and affirmation based entirely on performance, often complete with candy prizes for achievement and public humiliation for failure. Giving up these tactics might make us feel like we are being stripped of our tool belt. How will we get our students to do anything without exerting this kind of pressure? Again, the basic point is trust. If we actually appreciate our students, knowing that they possess intrinsic warmth and intelligence, but also that they are invested in their fearful minds, we can be truthful as well as kind. We can offer encouragement for their accomplishments without bloating them and setting them above others. We can reflect clearly on their challenges without demeaning their spirit.

Helping students rediscover their own inherent dignity is our real job. We might have to keep it a secret, but this is more important than teaching them reading, math, science, or anything else. How we do it is by creating a culture of genuine kindness. This is difficult even with a whole community of like-minded people, and we may have to tackle it all by ourselves. But what else is worth doing? Even if this approach yields lower grades, if it allows some students to feel like they could exist—could taste their own worthiness, even just a little bit—it will be worth it.

Curiosity

When it grows older,
With various displays of phenomena,
Lead it to the self-existing playground.

Once we have some sense of our human goodness and basic being, we naturally become curious. We relax the effort of fearfulness—that whole claustrophobic project of self-protection—and therefore we are able to look out and survey the world around us. We may feel as though we haven't noticed it before, and suddenly there is fresh air and a garden, a wondrous display of phenomena, there before us. We are drawn quite naturally toward it. We want to take off our shoes and walk around in it.

Curiosity is the Tao of learning. With curiosity, learning is like play, and we move towards it like children running out for recess. We have a natural wish to learn, to move our bodies and minds, to stretch, and to explore. For us as teachers, this curiosity might include an interest in our students, who display themselves in myriad ways. Rather than feeling terrified of them, we are interested in how we can play together, each in our respective roles. If one way of playing doesn't work, we can try another.

If we approach it with fresh eyes we will see the world as a self-existing playground. "Self-existing" means that it doesn't need our help to be interesting. The universe is a wondrous display of constantly changing energy. Things are what they are, independent of what we think or how we feel about them. They have their own potency and power. When we teach we are introducing our students to the world through "various displays of phenomena." These phenomena, whether they are letters, plants, concepts, calculations, games, stories, or anything else, are already brilliant. This is good news for us, because it means we don't have to sell our wares in the classroom. We can trust the beauty of our subjects to play with the curiosity of our students. We can trust the elegant precision of mathematics, the evocative drama of history, the natural wisdom of science, the stirring power of language arts, the pragmatism of health, and so on. A good teacher doesn't add interest, but finds creative ways to reveal the interesting facets of her subject. If we feel the need to "make it interesting," that indicates that we already think it's boring. We can put some lipstick on that pig, but after a while our little show runs out of steam. Let the pig be a self-existing pig and foster curiosity in the students. Then they will learn about the beauty of pigs, and it will be a job well done, whether they like it or not.

{ Confidence }

When it grows older still,
In order to promote the primordial confidence,
Lead it to the archery range of the warriors.

Learning leads to confidence. For example, if we learn to read then we feel confident picking up a book. However, in this case we are not talking about conventional learning, and therefore we are not talking about conventional confidence. We are learning about having true confidence in our minds and hearts. This confidence is primordial, meaning it resides in our being before we doubt ourselves. Discovering this confidence comes when we unlearn our habits of self-doubt, and we find that our human goodness is not fragile. Our being is not built up on a heap of fake credentials. When we have learned to trust deeply in our own being, we discover a confidence that is profound and real and makes us smile.

The archery range is a level beyond the playground. Having discovered some inkling of wellbeing in ourselves and some curiosity and playfulness with our world, we are ready for a further developmental step. We take up the bow and arrow, the martial tools of further training. This is like entering the classroom to teach. On the archery range, we may hit the target, or we may miss the target, we may drop the arrow, or we may shoot it into the ground. Further, the string of the bow may catch our ear or snap against our wrist. Our discipline, like our classroom, gives us constant feedback.

In Zen archery practice, one is instructed to shoot at the target, but informed that hitting the target is not the goal. The goal is to recognize your state of mind. Therefore, whatever happens with your arrow, the target becomes a mirror for your mind. Similarly, whatever happens with your lesson plan, the classroom becomes a mirror for your mind. In the process of giving birth to confidence, we are learning to let go of reference points. Our conventional confidence wants to prove itself by hitting the target every time. When we hit it, we are elated. When we miss, we are disappointed. But primordial confidence remains open, clear, and present no matter what happens. We can learn from hitting or missing the target without getting hung up on it. Sometimes we see this quality in a very senior teacher, one who has had many years and generations of students, or in a grandmother whose experience reflects a relaxed demeanor—warm, but unimpressed by any kind of drama.

This kind of confidence is the wellspring of compassion. Having honed our beings on the whetstone of the classroom and discovered that our heart of goodness is not fickle, we are able to care for our students from a place that is open and brave, not wincing or calculating. This is a very profound and mature discovery. Nevertheless, even if we still feel somewhat immature, we can discover it. We can see our students catching glimpses of it as well. As they grow and learn, they are no longer destroyed by their mistakes or carried away by their achievements. They may even begin to enjoy camaraderie and competition in a way that isn't mean, but draws out more energy. They are becoming warriors, which in the Shambhala tradition does not mean war-makers, but rather, those who are brave enough to be themselves without fear or aggression.

Dignity

When it grows older still,
To awaken primordial self-nature,
Let it see human society
Which possesses beauty and dignity.

When we let our noble qualities emerge, we shine. We feel good and that has a natural dignity that allows us to appreciate the interdependence of society. Being with others invokes possibilities of further learning and beauty. Rather than indulging in our individualism, we enjoy being a part of society.

Obviously, modern society has a lot of problems. Due to biases based on class, race, gender, sexual orientation, and ability, not everyone is given a safe, healthy, just basis for existing. We should get the training we need to work against these patterns as much as we can, rather than blindly replicating them in our classrooms. At the same time, we can recognize that dignity in society is always available. It does not come about as a result of material wealth or status alone. Rather, dignity is the product of confidence in human goodness. Therefore, we can foster dignity and create good society among any group of humans. Even three-year-olds can sit in a circle or at a table and manifest a society of great dignity, enjoying themselves and each other with crackers and grapes.

Having a sense of our place among others is like sitting down in a forest and touching the earth. Feeling and appreciating the elements, the earth and water, the air and the sun, we don't try to compete with them. We become a part of it. Whether we are teaching a class, attending a meeting, or having tea with a friend, we are creating and becoming beautiful society in that moment.

These levels of learning unfold and blossom organically as we move from a fearful mind to a fearless state of being, but again, the journey is more cyclical than linear. No matter what age we are or what our experience, we can find ourselves once again ensconced in fear, doubting our basic worth, grasping at habits of aggression, pride, and laziness. Then we need to start where we are. Once again, we meet ourselves with gentleness and trust, the cradle of loving-kindness. If we have never created the ground of care for ourselves, trying to develop confidence and dignity will be futile. Similarly, when our students express the many variations of fearful mind, regardless of their age, they need to be embraced with the discipline of gentleness and kindness until a sense of trust arises. The simplicity of trust allows curiosity to emerge. Curiosity leads to confidence, and confidence to dignity.

Mastery

Then the fearful mind
Can change into the warrior's mind,
And that eternally youthful confidence
Can expand into space without beginning or end.
At that point it sees the Great Eastern Sun.[27]

With a brave mind our confidence is eternally youthful because it has returned to innocence. Our glittering eyes reflect the magic that shimmers all around us, revealing the secret of life that can't be put into words. We don't have to learn or teach anything. We just enjoy being in the world, which is our continuous learning, and through simply being, we continuously teach. Every moment that arises in the classroom is brilliant and full of possibility, like the morning sun.

Conclusion

"In this place warmth and compassion mend the faint of heart, and quiet voices turn to tiger's roars...What has been pregnant in timid souls becomes fierce love in action, ready to take flight and change the world."–Nick, grade 12 graduation poem

Have you seen the Dunkin' Donuts commercial where the guy gets up early in the morning and stumbles off to work, day after day, mumbling, "Time to make the donuts"? I always liked that dude for some reason. There's something great about just doing our job in a matter-of-fact way, no big deal. I'm writing these last paragraphs at the end of summer. The days are long. Tomatoes are just turning red. The children are tanned and slightly feral. School will begin again soon. Time to teach the students. I'm a bit reluctant—I like summer break. But I'm also looking forward to it. This last year felt like a carnival of disasters and disturbing trends in world events. Those of us who care for the world are being called to meaningful work, and teaching is meaningful work. It's not a humdrum job. It's a way that, with a spark of inspiration, we can serve our world in a simple but crucial way.

That spark of inspiration isn't optional, though. Teaching is an art of feeling. All the feelings of our globalized world flow through the hearts and minds of each child. The blood of the world pulses through our interaction with each student. It takes a strong and deeply alive person to meet all those feelings without shrinking away. If we have doubt in our minds about the basic character of humanity, that doubt is like a fork in the road—it offers no guidance.

So, dear teacher, have no doubt. Your mind is good; invite it to be clear. Your body is good; invite it to be present. Your heart is good; invite it to be open. Your students are good; invite them to be themselves. Then the spark of goodness will ignite your teaching and breathe warmth and life into the world.

Acknowledgments

I am forever grateful to the Druk Sakyong, Chögyam Trungpa Rinpoche, whose bravery and compassion brought Shambhala to the world, and to my teacher Sakyong Mipham Rinpoche, who said, "You should write a book about education." The vision and wisdom within this book are attributed entirely to them. The half-baked parts are my own.

For raising me to be a warrior, my deep love and thanks to my parents and step-parents, Barbara and Mike Smith, Michael and Anne McLellan, and Danny Mann.

For loving encouragement and countless porch conversations, my deep thanks to Marguerite Drescher, and for constant disruption and inspiration, love and gratitude to our children, Gabriel and Esmé.

Thanks to my outstanding teachers along the way: everyone who worked at Vidya Elementary, which inspired me to teach, especially Linda Lewis and Richard Visser; from Casey Jr. High, John Williams; and lots of others. Also, a heartfelt salute to James Lowrey, Will Ryken, Mitchell Levy and the rest of the Shambhala Sun Camp Clan.

I'm deeply grateful to the staff of the Shambhala School, in particular to Steve Mustain for taking a risk on me, and to Jane Hester for being a genuine mentor.

For generous and practical advice in the process of writing this book, warm thanks to Emily Bower, Gaylon Ferguson, Judith Simmer-Brown, Emily Sell, Gabrielle Donnelly, Christopher Mazura, Susan Piver, and Carolyn Mandelker. Also thanks to the Teaching from the Heart team: Tony Cape, D'Arcy Colby, Tuyet Cullen, and Alexander DeVaron.

For the supportive, insightful, and skillful editing of this book, many thanks to Claire Zimmerman.

And thanks to all of my students over the years. Yes, I remember you.

About the Author

Noel McLellan is a school teacher and a meditation instructor. He is an acharya, or "honoured teacher," in the Shambhala tradition. He began practicing meditation when he was 12, and has trained in a variety of contemplative arts including Japanese archery, flower arranging, and calligraphy. Noel teaches middle and high school English and History and has served as Head Teacher as well as Dean of Mindfulness and Contemplative Learning. He has two children, Gabriel and Esmé, and lives in Halifax, Nova Scotia.

Notes

1   Chögyam Trungpa, *Shambhala, The Sacred Path of the Warrior*, pg. 89.

2   Naropa Commencement Address 2015. http://www.couragerenewal. org/living-from-the-inside-out-parker-palmers-naropa-u niversity-commencement-address. Accessed June 12, 2015.

3   https://www.nytimes.com/2015/04/07/nyregion/at-success-academ y-charter-schools-polarizing-methods-and-superior-results.html, accessed April 6, 2015.

4   Rachael Kessler, "Soul of Students, Soul of Teachers," from *Schools with Spirit, Nurturing the Inner Lives of Children and Teachers*, pg's 121-122.

5   Trungpa, pg. 44

6   John Stevens, *Dewdrops on a Lotus Leaf: Zen Poems of Ryokan.*

7   M.K. Asante, *Buck*, pg. 200.

8   I mostly teach in a classroom, with desks and chairs. I even use chalk (old school!). But of course our classroom might be a basketball court, a forest, a dojo, a boat, etc.

9   This analogy comes from my meditation teacher, Sakyong Mipham Rinpoche, author of *Turning the Mind Into An Ally.*

10 William James, *The Principles of Psychology, Vol. 1*, pg. 424.

11 Another wonderful analogy from Sakyong Mipham Rinpoche.

12 Instructions from a book are good, but if possible, seek out meditation instruction from a qualified teacher in person or online.

13 In her book *Building A Better Teacher*, Elizabeth Green explores what she calls "the myth of the natural-born teacher," the pervasive idea that great teaching is a product of personality traits rather than learnable skills, and how this idea actually isolates teachers and ensures that

teaching as a profession does not improve. *Building A Better Teacher*, Elizabeth Green, pg.'s 1-21.

[14] David Booth and Masayuki Hachiya, editors, *The Arts Go To School*, pg. 14.

[15] Richard Brown's article *The Mindful Teacher as the Foundation of Contemplative Pedagogy* has further helpful advice for bringing our mindfulness practice into the classroom. Published in *Meditation and the Classroom: Contemplative Pedagogy for Religious Studies*, by Judith Simmer-Brown and Fran Grace. The article is also available online.

[16] As Orestes Brownson said in the 19th century, "Education, such as it is, is ever going on. Our children are educated in the streets, by the influence of their associates... in the bosom of the family, by the love and gentleness or wrath and fretfulness of parents, by the passions or affections they see manifested, the conversations to which they listen, and above all by the general pursuits, habits, and moral tone of the community. In all these are schoolrooms and schoolmaster sending forth scholars educated for good or for evil or, what is more likely, for a little of both. The real question for us to ask is not, Shall our children be educated? but, To what end shall they be educated, and by what means? What is the kind of education needed, and how shall it be furnished?" (from Dana Goldstein, *The Teacher Wars*, pg. 31)

[17] "Caring Without Tiring; Dealing with compassion fatigue burnout in teaching." *Education Canada*. http://www.cea-ace.ca/education-canada/article/caring-without-tiring. Accessed September 10, 2016.

[18] "Compassion Fatigue; Bodily symptoms of empathy." *Psychology Today*. https://www.psychologytoday.com/blog/somatic-psychology/201207/compassion-fatigue. Accessed September 10, 2016.

[19] Chögyam Trungpa, *The Collected Works of Chögyam Trungpa, vol.4*, pg. 635.

[20] "John Dewy Quotes." http://www.quotes.net/quote/50699. Accessed March 31, 2016.

[21] Parker Palmer, Naropa Commencement Address 2015. http://www.couragerenewal.org/living-from-the-inside-out-parker-palmers-naropa-university-commencement-address/. Accessed June 12, 2015

22 For a clear and interesting description of this process I recommend the first chapter of *Hold On To Your Kids*, by Gabor Maté and Gordon Neufeld.

23 With gratitude to Vaughan Doucette for sharing this reflection. (Included with permission)

24 Sun Tzu, *The Art of War, The Denma Translation*, pg. 155.

25 There are many translations of *The Art of War*. I recommend *The Rules of Victory: How to Transform Chaos and Conflict—Strategies from the Art of War*, by James Gimian and Barry Boyce.

26 "A Public Dialogue Between bell and hooks and Cornell West," https://www.youtube.com/watch?v=_LL0k6_pPKw, accessed July 1, 2016

27 Trungpa, *Shambhala, the Sacred Path of the Warrior*, pg. 89

CPSIA information can be obtained
at www.ICGtesting.com
Printed in the USA
FSHW011840220619
59330FS